SMALL WONDERS

Small Wonders

Stories of Love, Loss and Letting Go

ANNE THURSTON

VERITAS

Published 2014 by
Veritas Publications
7–8 Lower Abbey Street
Dublin 1, Ireland

publications@veritas.ie
www.veritas.ie

ISBN 978-1-84730-574-9

Designed by Lir Mac Cárthaigh, Veritas Publications
Printed in Ireland by Watermans Printers Ltd, Cork

Veritas books are printed on paper made from the wood pulp of managed forests. For every tree felled, at least one tree is planted, thereby renewing natural resources.

Acknowledgements

THE IMPETUS TO WRITE THESE BRIEF REFLECTIONS CAME from requests to contribute to several series of *A Living Word* for RTÉ Radio 1 over a number of years. New pieces have been added, some of which appeared originally in short essays for a column entitled 'Thinking Aloud' in the journal, *Reality*. All have been revised for this collection. I thank Aidan Mathews, producer of *A Living Word*, for his courteous reception of my work and his constant encouragement to have the 'small pieces', broadcast in the 'small hours', published. For bringing that forward, I owe a debt to Donna Doherty, commissioning editor of Veritas. I thank her and the whole publication team, in particular designer Lir Mac Cárthaigh for a cover that so beautifully visualises the contents.

My family of past, present and future generations has been a source of inspiration for this work. My parents, Nuala and Tony Meldon, are recalled with love and gratitude, my children, Katie, Lucy and Dominic, two of whom are now parents themselves, will find traces of their lives in these pages, and the three 'small wonders' – our grandchildren, Evie, Imogen and George – are the most recent source of joy punctuating these reflections.

Finally, as always, I thank my companion and husband Timothy, who has shared all these stories of love, of loss, of letting go.

Contents

Introduction

AS THE BOOK'S COVER SUGGESTS, WHAT THE READER FINDS
here is a tableau of images and memories. The small essays
are loosely gathered according to themes which have
emerged, but the order is not precise or even important
in terms of how one reads them.

As I have drawn them together I have more the sense
of a patchwork quilt than a seamless garment. They come
from the bits and pieces of life's experiences over the past
fifteen years. Just as one chooses such patches for their
contrasting colours of light and dark, of pattern and plain,
so these pieces register joy and sorrow, wonder and wounds,
grief and grace – sometimes altogether. Thirty and more
years ago my life was shaped very strongly by the births
of my three children, and twelve years ago marked deeply
both by the deaths of my parents and the simultaneous
coming to adulthood of those children. In the between-
time of my mid-life I noted how loss and liberation shaped
that space and how love was often defined by 'letting go'.
Five years ago I returned to academic study and completed
a PhD in Theology. Now I am at a different stage, that of

grandparenthood, and the cycle of births begins again: the first grandchild erupted joyfully into our lives two years ago. Now there are three.

What I have recorded here are ordinary moments registering some of these events. For different reasons they have become small epiphanies, occasions for wonder. I have not drawn any clear lines of separation between the more overtly religious and the apparently secular pieces. I see them as part of the same pattern of incarnation which does not seek for things of the spirit outside of earth and flesh, but instead searches the depths of matter for the luminous, the numinous. Some of these stories are illustrations of such 'breaking through', ruptures of grace into and out of experience. For this reason too, the dark places of sorrow or ambiguity are not avoided or glossed over but struggled with until the reader or writer emerges bearing both wound and blessing.

ANNE THURSTON
September 2014

LOVE, LOSS AND LETTING GO

Many of these pieces were written after the deaths of my parents. Only after some time has passed is one fully aware of the impact of such events. I find myself, even now twelve to fourteen years later, surprised by the feelings and memories they evoke. They remain fertile ground for imagination and thought. It seemed fitting to include birth stories in this section too, not least because both involve dark passageways and long journeys. They seemed to follow quite naturally as the cycle of love and letting go begins again.

Birth and death

I CAN REMEMBER THE FINAL WEEKS AND THEN THE DAYS before the birth of my first child. I was excited and nervous, eagerly awaiting the birth and yet terrified that I wouldn't be able to cope with this child who would be totally dependent on us for her every need. Once she arrived we wouldn't be able to hand her back. Nothing quite prepares one for this profound upheaval. The birth of a child changes everything.

When that first child was on the cusp of adulthood I found myself waiting for death. We were lucky – the death of a parent in their eighties is sad but not tragic. It is not a life snatched away before it has been allowed to flower and fade, but a life reaching its natural end. Yet there is the absolute finality of death. The line between presence and absence is not blurred; it is the sharpest line of all. Death changes everything.

Poet and undertaker Thomas Lynch is a wise observer of the facts of death. These, he says, are as important to learn as the facts of life. We are so practised in the arts of avoidance we seek to minimise the pain, but as he observes, the truth is a better healer than 'fiction or fantasy'.*

The youngest family members were for us the healers and the truth-tellers. 'Will they put the earth in with their hands or with a digger?' asked the three year old as he stood at the graveside, and some days later, when we stumbled over the words, 'Let's go to Granny and ..., I mean, Granddad's house', he quickly retorted, 'Not Granny, silly – Granny is dead.'

Now I think I know what midlife is: it is this space between those two life-defining realities of birth and death. They looked oddly similar too, with the pain and the struggle preceding the letting go. The benediction for the arriving child and the valediction for the departing parent were also similar: the kiss and the assurance, 'Everything will be alright'.

* From his 'The Way We Were' in *Bodies in Motion and at Rest* (London: Jonathan Cape, 2000), 79

The dance of resurrection

'THE DEAD GRANDDAD IS IN HERE,' SAID THE FOUR YEAR old as he pointed the way for the friends and relations coming to the wake of his great-grandfather.

The next day at the funeral the priest, who clearly knew the ninety-year-old farmer very well, spoke warmly about him. First, with great delicacy he told the widow that he wasn't going to 'interfere with her sorrow'. He clearly didn't intend to offer clichéd words of comfort nor say such things as 'time will heal' or even 'he's in a better place'. For the priest knew full well that for her there was no 'better place' than by her side. He understood that resurrection faith is a slow dawning rather than a quick fix.

The farmer was renowned as an Irish dancer and people came from far and wide to ask his advice about their steps. And even when he had lost his sight and was blind for the latter years of his life, he could still listen for the steps of the dances he knew so well. He was, it seemed, attuned to what was going on and not just to the traditional songs and dances, but also to the sounds of the land, the river, the sea.

His body was taken to the old parish graveyard to be entombed rather than placed in the ground, as is the tradition for many families in that part of the country. After the coffin had been carefully inserted into place and the small door closed behind it, we heard the sound of men singing and playing the accordion. There were ballads from Kerry and Connemara. On the slab outside the grave there was a clearing on which a board had been laid, and two women got up to dance. They danced the steps they had learnt from their mentor. 'Dancing on my grave' took on a whole new meaning. Here the dance celebrated a life; it honoured the dead; it wove a seamless connection between those living and those departed. The priest who had led the mourners in a decade of the rosary looked on and smiled because he knew that the rhythms of the prayers just said and the steps of the dance were all signs of resurrection faith.

There were no more speeches, no graveside orations, just the simple prayers, the singing and the dancing.

It seemed to us 'townies', watching this funeral of the father of our brother-in-law, that we were the ones cut off from the rhythm of life, the rhythm of death. We were the ones most ignorant of the facts of death. They looked death in the face and were not afraid.

Letting go

A DAUGHTER GRADUATED FROM COLLEGE IN THE SUMMER after the death of my mother in the spring, and left for Australia in the autumn. As we moved into the short dark days of winter we were learning about letting go.

The last remnants of childhood would be shaken off and an adult would return. The graduation ceremony in the college is called Commencements. What to us seemed like an ending was of course also a beginning. As we watched our happy smiling daughter, we were aware that these years had made her wiser in more ways than the writing of essays and the preparation of projects. She had danced across the cobblestones at the Trinity Ball, and probably stumbled across them fighting back tears at the end of a relationship or the betrayal of a friend. She had been stimulated and bored by lecturers. She had tried and tested many things and had learned her own limits.

And in this, her final year, she had seen her grandmother die. Her grandfather came alone to watch his granddaughter, his camera as usual around his neck. Eager to get there, he slipped and fell. He insisted on carrying on, and the following day delivered one of his best black and white photos of a radiant granddaughter.

Now I look at that photo, of a laughing daughter and proud parents at her commencements ceremony. We wished so much for her, for her siblings, her peers, for their future, their happiness. But there was also the realisation that we could not, and did not, make things perfect for them, or even always alright again. We had to let go and trust.

All Souls' Day

MY FATHER HAD BEEN IN HOSPITAL SINCE SEPTEMBER AND the days were punctuated with visits there and anxious conversations with brothers and sisters. My mother had died eighteen months previously and, by a cruel twist of fate, my father had been diagnosed with the very condition from which she had died. Although surgery had been successful, he seemed unable to deal with the trauma of finding himself in the same hospital under the same surgeons as she had been; it was like a bad dream from which, it appeared, he didn't want to wake.

During that autumn and winter of his illness there were, ironically, some of the most beautiful and bright days that I can remember.

The second of November was one such day. I decided to visit my mother's grave. I was carrying a brown paper bag filled with bulbs: snowdrops, grape hyacinths, crocuses and bluebells. On the grave the seed heads from a summer flowering of love-in-the-mist were still there. I shook out the remaining seeds and thought of how my mother loved those flowers, with their soft blue held in a sea of feathery green.

As I weeded and prepared the earth for planting, I remembered my mother and prayed for my father. It felt good to be there planting bulbs and creating a garden. I thought of how life comes out of death.

Although there is a long-standing tradition in some parts of the country of visiting graves in November, particularly on that day, I had never done so before, imagining it to be a somewhat morbid exercise. I belong to a generation and culture where death is the last taboo. But as I worked with the earth that held the remains of my mother I felt no fear, but rather a new surge of hope and trust. I felt sure that I would be returning in the spring to see the bulbs flower and not to disturb the earth for another burial.

Losing and keeping

'OF NO MONETARY VALUE,' THE EXPERT HAD SAID, AS IF that settled the matter of their disposal.

Little did he know! These small things grew in importance as we cleared the family home after the death of our parents. A photograph on the mantelpiece, a cracked jug, an old box, a book with its cover missing were all as hotly contested, as desirable, as antiques in an auction room.

They were now freighted with a significance which they did not have some weeks before and which they would not have some weeks hence. But for now they were precious to us.

Our struggle to gain possession of these bits and pieces of our parents' lives, and of our childhood past, were marked by ancient rivalries, as in our family home we became again the children we once were, vying for attention, seeking to establish our places of affection and importance. Relinquishing claims became another form of letting go.

In time these things will lose that gloss, or will themselves be lost, and the angel with the chipped wing given to me by Miss McKillop on my First Communion Day will lie forgotten in a drawer, until, in turn, our children come to clear our clutter.

As poet, Dennis O'Driscoll, wisely commented, 'All these things we hoard as adults ... will become lost property eventually too. It will die on us or we will die on it.'*

But for now these paltry things have become part of our inheritance, ciphers of a life that we hold now only in story and memory, a memory awakened by seeing again that cloth taken out when visitors came, or that bowl in which bread was mixed, or that photograph with the scribble 'Achill 1947' on the back, where the story first began.

* From an essay entitled 'Losers, Weepers: Christian Boltanski's *Lost Property*', published in *Troubled Thoughts, Majestic Dreams: Selected Prose Writing* (Meath: The Gallery Press, 2001), 360

A family house

'THE HOUSE IS TOO CLUTTERED. YOU'LL HAVE TO CLEAR some of it before selling,' the auctioneer said.

So we moved in and swooped down, vulture-like, on what we wanted, cleaning and clearing, sorting and giving away, until the house began to resemble what passes for suburban comfort, if far from postmodern chic. 'The *lived-in* look is what we want' – as if a house lived in and out of for fifty years could have any other look.

We cut the grass and weeded the beds, we filled the rooms with flowers and placed pictures and chairs strategically, to conceal what we now judged to be worn and shabby, and thus we saw our family home become 'a house with potential'. The silver birch that my father gave to my mother for their twenty-fifth wedding anniversary is now part of 'a south-facing garden with mature shrubs and trees'. My mother's old gardening shoes are long gone.

Now the 'Sold' sign hangs, almost accusingly, the grass has grown long again and the house, stripped nearly bare, has become a place of ghosts, and it is painful to go in to collect the last bits and pieces. Only the leaves of the birch tree shimmer as shards of sun cut through the raindrops.

The picture of the Sacred Heart that hung in the bedroom now lies abandoned against the kitchen table. The papal blessing gets a reprieve, being moved to the box marked 'archive stuff', where it will sit with diaries revealing Protestant bishops among our ancestors, a kind of post-mortem ecumenism.

As for the rest, the last remaining bits and pieces that nobody wants, they will be bagged, binned or burnt.

'Till death do us part

MY FATHER RESISTED ALL ATTEMPTS TO GET HIM TO change from his beloved black and white photography to colour film, and he continued to bring his camera to every family gathering and to develop his own pictures until some months before he died. Now we are glad he resisted colour snaps – to say nothing of digital pictures – as these boxes and boxes of his photos carry a lifetime of memories, all the more evocative in the light and the shadow of the black and white.

We scour them for stories – that slim woman picking flowers under the trees in Wicklow gardens would later become our mother. That same woman smiles out at the camera again and again over the next fifty-two years they will spend together. They were years not unmarked by pain and sorrow, strain and difficulty, and yet it seemed that each time she stood again under some tree or beside a lake or near the sea, she was once more that young woman being wooed by the handsome photographer.

So we should not have been surprised when, after my mother's death, two years before his own, my father reframed some of his early photos of her, placing them alongside others taken with children and grandchildren. It was then we were jolted into the recognition that these two – parents of seven and grandparents of eighteen – were in the first place, and indeed the last, lovers.

Love letters

WHEN MY MOTHER DIED MY FATHER DESTROYED HIS LOVE letters to her. They had been treasured by her, but were not for us to read. There was only one he permitted us to see because it illustrated something about how communication worked in the days before email, text and, in their case, even a house phone.

He had left the house early for work, as was his habit, but had failed to part with the usual kiss. Perhaps they had an argument the night before, left unresolved by one of his, not untypical, silences. When he reached the office he felt remorseful and sent my mother a postcard with a 'sorry' and with his love. The plain white card reached her by the afternoon post that same day.

My father was hopeless at giving gifts. Even now I can see the disappointment on my mother's face at every birthday as she unwrapped something he thought clever or suitable or practical. They were certainly never what one would call 'romantic' gifts. There was a glass weight shaped like a pineapple. Did she even like pineapples? There was a tea set decorated with pheasants: she certainly didn't care for pheasants.

Yet his written messages accompanying those gifts, however brief or cryptic, were full of tenderness. Often the birthday card would be a photograph he had taken. He photographed my mother all her life and I think in every picture he took he continued to see the beautiful young woman with whom he had fallen in love, and to whom he wrote, 'Sorry I left without saying goodbye this morning. Love, Tony', on a postcard that we can still hold in our hands.

The facts of death

'I AM WRITING NOW THAT YOU ARE ORPHANS' WAS THE opening line of the letter from a family friend. How odd I thought. 'Orphan' seemed hardly appropriate to describe forty and fifty year olds even if they had lost their parents.

What does stop us in our tracks is the realisation that there is now nothing between us and the grave. At some stage when we were children someone took us aside – usually behind closed doors – to explain what were called 'the facts of life'. But some of us don't learn the 'facts of death' until we stand at our parents' graveside – and for this there is no dress rehearsal.

If we are blessed to be granted the time span of our own parents we will continue to protect our children and in turn will cradle theirs. But it is still we who are next.

However, there is another sense in which perhaps orphan *is* the right word. That process of letting go which began at birth is completed at death. There is a freedom granted with the death of one's parents and not just from the burden of care – though there is that too – but a freedom to move into a larger space, a freedom in some way to be more fully ourselves. This is perhaps their most important legacy, their last gift, and I am happy to have received it, and not left it unopened, unrecognised at the graveside.

Old hands

A DAUGHTER REMEMBERS HER GRANDMOTHERS BY THEIR hands.

One had large hands that took your face and held it. It was a gesture warm, knowing and comforting. You were held, you were seen, and you were loved.

The other had the knotted, gnarled hands of one suffering from some arthritic condition. They didn't grasp your face but held your hand in theirs, stroking it, talking to it. The fingernails of the first hands were clean and worn; the fingers told of the years of hard labour of child rearing, of washing clothes by hand until an aunt, who bet on horses and smoked Craven A, and never washed her own clothes, gave some money for the purchase of an automatic washing machine. These were hands that had been covered in flour as they swiftly kneaded a brown loaf and put it in the oven.

The fingernails on the arthritic hands were carefully buffed and polished, and the hands, though twisted, retained, if not a beauty then a memory of beauty, and certainly a pride. These hands could arrange flowers with a skill that turned a simple bunch of spring daffodils into an art form. In the last days those hands clawed the sheets searching for the silk ribbon that once bordered them, but silk-bordered sheets are not hospital issue.

The large hands of the other grandmother lay unresponsive by her side; each day my father took one of them in his and hoped for some sign that she knew he was there.

In both cases they took the rings off, first the swollen, and then – when her turn came – the bony fingers, and gave them to us. I keep them for the granddaughter who, when she remembers her grandmothers, remembers their hands.

Expecting

WHEN I WAS A CHILD THE WORD 'PREGNANT' WAS NEVER used. A modesty veil of language covered all bodily matters. I stood next to my mother as she chatted to friends, curious as to what Mary might be 'expecting' – a parcel was the most likely, I thought, wrapped in brown paper, tied with string, coming from Toronto or Boston, to be kept hidden away until Christmas.

The writers of the Hebrew scriptures tell endless stories about births. There are stories · of annunciations and visitations. Angels come – sometimes in disguise – and are entertained as they bring news of impending births. So much for planned pregnancies, and yet every birth is seen as part of the Creator's plan. 'Before you were born I knew you.'

It may seem odd at first that almost all of the births recounted are in some way out of time, out of place. Births come to women who are barren like Hannah, or to women past child-bearing age like Sarah or Elizabeth. The news is usually greeted with shock, with disbelief or even with laughter. But by drawing our attention to the unusual, the storytellers highlight the ordinary as graced. It is not the barrenness of Elizabeth nor the old age of Sarah nor even the virginity of Mary that matters most, but the surprise and gift of every birth, the reminder that life is not ours to control, to take as right, but to receive with thanks and praise, this commonplace miracle.

One day some springtime past I was having tea with an expectant grandmother when the phone rang. Her daughter announced the birth of her own longed-for daughter, and as the newborn cry broke over the waves, an echoing cry of gratitude, a vernacular *Magnificat*, sounded in the room and the air grew light as the universe made way for this new child.

A child is born

'UNTO US A CHILD IS BORN.' DESPITE EVERY EFFORT TO sanitise it, or capture it in theological formulae, or contain it in historical or scientific explanation, despite the worst excesses of the commercial world to make it tawdry, despite the sentimentality, the glitter and the tinsel, there is something about the mystery of this birth that overwhelms us.

The most hardened secularists are found at the back of churches on Christmas Eve singing familiar carols with tears, not entirely induced by mulled wine, filling their eyes.

There is of course nostalgia here, but there is something else.

With every birth there is a struggle, a well-named labour and then the release of fierce and tender love. There is something about the vulnerability of every newborn child that awakens in us the deep desire to protect life.

The Christian conviction of a God made vulnerable, flesh of our flesh, that we might be sister and brother to one another's need, touches us profoundly. There is something that we reach for each time we witness or remember or celebrate birth, something that defies our cynicism and rekindles our hope.

So we come out on the darkest and longest of winter nights, despite, or perhaps because of, the darkness and confusion in our own hearts.

We come just for one moment, in this frenetic time, not to grasp but to be grasped by the mystery of word made flesh.

Praise poem for infants

For it was you who formed my inmost parts
You knit me together in my mother's womb
I praise you for I am fearfully and wonderfully
*   made.*

—PSALM 139

THE POET OF THIS PSALM CAPTURES THE DELICACY AND intricacy of the human form that usually causes us to catch our breath when we first look at a new baby. We nervously reach out and place a clumsy finger in a tiny and perfect hand and are amazed when the small fingers curl round and grasp ours. We gaze with awe at the fragility and vulnerability of new life. The child breathes, life is given. There is nothing more extraordinary than this ordinary wonder.

Our daughter and her husband bring their new baby home to introduce her to her two-year-old sister. We, the grandparents, slip away to allow this encounter to take place. Later we receive a set of pictures and videos. The scene is so gently and beautifully choreographed: at first the new infant is lying in the pram and her big sister peeps in. Then her father holds the new baby and her older sister sits next to him looking with great seriousness as they have a conversation and speak her name. Then her mother takes the baby, and their first-born moves closer to gaze with wonder at this living being. First she takes up one tiny hand and examines it, and then reaches over and takes up the other hand and checks it too, and then does the same with her feet, and looks at her mother and announces that the baby is out now. As I look at the pictures of this precious encounter, in her gaze I see the words of the psalmist in a slightly different register: 'For it was you who formed her inward parts;/you knit her together in her mother's womb./I praise you for she is fearfully and wonderfully made.'

Baby talk

IT IS ODD WHEN YOU THINK ABOUT IT THAT THE NOTION of the autonomous self took such a hold. The virtue of appearing strong and independent, the hero vanquishing the dragon, the winner taking all, the cowboy riding into the sunset ... these predominantly male myths miss the mark.

The philosopher Mary Midgley has a gentler take on how we are as human beings. She notes that human babies recognise and respond to other people before they know themselves.* It takes time before a small child looking in the mirror can say 'me, me' – then of course they never stop! But to know the face of the mother, or father, or grandparent before they know themselves, suggests that we are made *first* for relationship. And there is no 'me, me' without a responding 'you, you'. Others call us by name and so we learn to know ourselves. Young couples are rightly proud when their first child arrives, but it is the child who 'makes' them parents, and makes them flush with pride at the first 'mama', 'dada'. In our western world we define 'growing up' as 'independence' – as moving away – but in other places it might be understood as learning responsibility for those who have nurtured us, and as giving back to the community from which we have come. So the child held between the mother and father's arms learning to walk will later take hold of her parents' arms and aid their faltering steps.

—◦◦✝◦◦—

* From her *Science and Poetry* (London and New York: Routledge Classics, 2001), 125

A human face

IN MARILYNNE ROBINSON'S NOVEL *GILEAD*, THE PASTOR John Ames speaks about the faces of the infants he baptises, and how he feels that each one is a blessing:

> There is nothing more astonishing than a human face ... it has something to do with incarnation. You feel your obligation to a child when you have seen it and held it. Any human face is a claim on you, because you can't help but understand the singularity of it, the courage and loneliness of it. But this is truest of the face of an infant.*

The baptism of our first grandchild was a chaotic affair, as these events can be, but the 'sacred' memory I carry is the way the child lay in her father's arms and did not take her eyes from his face. As I watched them, I thought, 'She is certainly making her claim on him'. Now at two years I see how she continues to read faces, alert to every change of expression and what it might mean. The philosopher Levinas speaks about the call of the human face as an ethical call, and Robinson gives this notion flesh: to hold an infant child and look at its face is to know such a call. As these small creatures reintroduce us both to the fragility and the wonder of human life, in turn we want to draw them in to the practices and rituals that have sustained and nourished our lives, made sense of its pains and its joys. And if the parents choose a sacramental life for their children you want them to do this because it seems that the urge to give thanks and praise after the birth of a child calls for a 'Thanks be to God' in some shape. Our own words always seem inadequate for these occasions, and the rhythms of something like Psalm 136, with its litany of 'for his steadfast love endures forever', places our thanksgiving into a cosmic context.

* London: Virago, 2004, 75

Original blessing

THE TWO NEW FATHERS SPOKE ABOUT THE EFFECT OF THE arrival of their children: one spoke of the gift of his adopted daughter: 'In our case this was made manifest by the fact that when they brought her to us, someone had tied a ribbon around her.' For these parents, who had waited a long time to receive their child, the joy was immense. It spilled over into a gratitude, which washed over the whole community. The other talked about the life-changing presence of his new son. 'You get no sleep,' he said, 'but you get back in spades what you have given.' 'He likes to wave,' informed this young father. 'If you see him waving, wave back.'

Both had the impulse to praise, the impulse to give thanks. They were here to tell us this. During the previous year they had brought their newly arrived children to this church for baptism – signifying their belonging to the communion of saints and sinners, the graced and flawed, who are the body of Christ in this place. Now they had returned to witness to the blessings received, to the grace poured out.

So when we were asked to raise our hands in blessing over them, we did so willingly. The child who liked to wave saw our hands in the air and waved to us, and when we applauded his father's words, he clapped his small hands in delight.

Not waving but blessing ...

Birth bruised and blessed

HE HOLDS THE SMALL, BIRTH-BRUISED AND CRUMPLED body of his newborn child.

She is so tiny she almost fits in the cradle he makes of his hands. He is overwhelmed by feelings he has never known. He wants to protect this child from every danger. He will love her no matter what assails her, ails her. She is utterly precious to him.

Until this moment prayer had been something abstract; now he mutters over and over, 'Thank you, thank you, thank you!'

A very little while later, they tell him that his daughter has Downs syndrome.

His prayer is now accompanied by tears, but he cannot wish her back, he cannot wish her otherwise.

It would be false to record that there was no anger and frustration in the tears. It would be wrong to pretend that there were no cries of 'Why us?'

Yet essentially the feelings he had before do not change. They intensify.

She is still grace, still gift.

He knows that they will be the ones who will need to change to make space for her difference.

There will be difficulties, there will be sorrow and heartbreak, there will be grieving for expectations unfulfilled. There will be unexpected delights. But for now there is nothing but this child who has arrived and who will depend on them for milk and kindness.

'This is our precious daughter,' he says, and holds her out in his arms.

Small world

IT WAS THE SMALL CHILD I NOTICED FIRST. I WAS ON A train travelling from Harrisburg in Pennsylvania to Penn station in New York. As I walked down the carriage the little girl smiled and I stopped to talk to her. I tend to talk to the recently arrived in the world and to encourage their young mothers. I think it's a grandmother's impulse (although at that stage I wasn't yet a biological grandmother), a kind of Anna or Simeon desire to pass on a blessing, and to receive one.

I got into conversation with the mother. 'Where are you from?' she asked. 'Dublin,' I replied. 'Oh,' she said,

'I was a student there for a time.' This young woman, born in Mumbai in India, now living in the UK, had been in Dublin to take International Peace Studies in Trinity College, Dublin.

Within seconds of meeting we are exchanging names of mutual acquaintances. She asks me to bring greetings. I tell her of my son's travels to India. Then we talk books, we talk motherhood, we talk Montessori learning ... two strangers momentarily brought into a web of connection, and not virtual either.

A random encounter on a train one Sunday in October in America and the world shrinks, or expands, to the size of this carriage – and three generations, two nationalities and three continents meet in the smile of a child.

Setting out

AS A NEW GRANDMOTHER I'M GETTING USED TO THE FLOW of images marking the child's progress. Smartphones now ensure that no moment is left unrecorded – pictures and even little videos arrive at regular intervals: the first smile, wave, crawl, the first steps, the first words and so on. And like all grandparents I am besotted and will bore anyone willing to look at them. As my daughter says, most parents and grandparents think their offspring is the most beautiful, the cleverest; we just know ours is!

However, among the many images in my album, there is a recent one that I've been thinking about. You don't see the child's face at all, so it may seem strange that I choose this one.

In the photo you see the back of the small – what I refer to as 'pint-sized' – child. She is walking away from the camera. In front of her stretches a long path; for her size it is a long, long road ahead. On her back she has a little rucksack shaped like a koala bear with a long tail. The tail is taut and held by an invisible hand, off camera. The child doesn't look back but is very clearly 'setting out'.

I love this image for all that it says about the pull of independence and the gentle unobtrusive sign of dependence ... the umbilical cord of the koala tail still attaching the child to her mother, who in a very wise move allows this sense of freedom while retaining a watchful eye, a careful oversight.

Parent and child are learning the most important lesson: letting go. This is the unending work of love: knowing when to hold close, and when to release, for the child is not ours to keep but simply to mind, until those early steps setting out on the path become the steps of her own journey and her own life.

BREATHING SPACE

After the death of my parents and the leaving home of our adult children, I experienced what I could best describe as a 'breathing space'; I recognised that the past years had been spent primarily in caring for others: first nurturing and bringing up our children, and then, as they aged, helping to mind elderly parents. In many ways I had chosen this part and seen it as 'good'. Now there was a 'space', how would I use it? What would I do? Was there a 'better part'? Would I find myself again, outside of the roles of 'mother', 'daughter', 'sister'? These seem to me to be important midlife questions. Could I re-imagine a spirit-life, a faith-life, a love-life in terms of liberation and not duty? What form would that take? This section only obliquely addresses some of these things but they hover around the pieces I have gathered here.

Advent dawning

*O Oriens, O daystar, come and illumine those who
sit in darkness and the shadow of death.*

Thus begins one of the 'O Antiphons', which mark the days
coming up to Christmas. This particular chant seems most
apt, coinciding as it does with the time of the winter solstice.

We had decided to go to Glendalough, pilgrimage
place of St Kevin, and spend one night away from the
panic of trying and failing to please and to party. This was
the first year for a long time that I was allowing myself to
draw breath and resist the pressure of expectations (my
own) to make everyone (else) happy for Christmas.

We arrive in winter sunlight. There is time for a walk
around the first lake with its banks of rusted bracken
and the unleafed trees with their thin tracery of branches
against the sky. We walk among the stones of the ancient
monastic settlement and step in the hollowed out and
hallowed spaces of the cathedral ruins.

A robin sings from a holly bush and we laugh at its
Christmas card posing. Suddenly the low sun gilds the
lake and we stop and draw breath. It is bitterly cold and
we go back to our cottage to light fires and candles and
have hot soup.

The following morning we wake early and go back to
the lake to watch the rising sun that marks the turning
from darkness to light.

A bird sings matins from the bare branches and the empty ruins.

And it dawns on me that attending to this bird and this place is all I need at this moment. We return home after just twenty-four hours, and on this occasion I manage to carry the calm through to Christmas.

Laughter lines

IN OUR YOUTH-OBSESSED CULTURE AGEING IS EMBARrassing, and so it is that wrinkles are erased, lines of sorrow, anger and even laughter are pressed out; bodies are toned in the gym and imperfections worked out.

But this is September: the leaves are beginning to turn and some even to fall; in my garden autumn is starting early after the unusually dry summer. Its gaudiness is fading, giving way to something mellow.

I speak to a photographer at a party. 'I love to take portraits of older people,' he says, 'the character in those faces is so much more interesting than the unlined and inexperienced faces of the young.' Perhaps we need a *Goodbye* magazine to balance *Hello!* and in place of the airbrushed and manicured pictures of the fixed smiles we would see faces marked with the pain and the joy of living, faces lined with laughter and longing, faces contorted by anger and grief, faces creased with surprise, wrinkled with winters and summers of accumulated wisdom and wit.

Midlife

THE MIRROR DOESN'T LIE, THEY SAY, BUT AH IT DOES. THE face you see when you wash and dress each morning is the same face as yesterday, and the day before, and the day before that: you see the same person. The surprise is that other people show their age! It is only in the unguarded moments when you catch sight of a reflection in a shop window or going down an escalator and a vaguely familiar face looks back, and you wonder, 'Who is that woman?' Caught off-guard and without the protection of the watchful ego, the face falls, and with a shock you see what others see: a middle-aged woman rushing home with her shopping, or her briefcase, and wondering what she will say at that meeting, or what she will cook for dinner tonight. The blush of youth has become the flush of the menopause.

You are shocked too that nowadays they are appointing mere school-leavers as university professors and hospital consultants. That young girl who has just walked in must be a student on work experience, but no, she takes your blood pressure and leaves instructions with the nurse who, reassuringly, looks older than you are (which probably means the same age). You take out your glasses to read not just the prescription but also the newspaper, the menu and the price tags, and you are irritated that everything seems to be in such small print these days. You seem to stand between the wise elders and the impossibly young successors who have already caught the ends of Elijah's cloak and are refashioning it.

How did you get here? It seems as if one day you were a student, then a young mother with children, and now a middle-aged woman whose adult children have all left home. You find yourself in a space between the nursery and the nursing home. Is this a narrow passageway, a one-way street ending in the grave, or is it a clearing where time takes on a different dimension?

Ah, the proverbial midlife crisis strikes and you ask yourself – what have I done with my life? What can I do now? Where am I going?

Breathing space

IT'S A FUNNY THING, THIS BUSINESS OF WAITING TO GROW up.

The first tastes of freedom in what we called a 'flat' were, despite that appellation, exhilarating. This was particularly so for me as we had views from sea to mountains to city. This 'penthouse' panorama came courtesy of a tiny roof space off a little kitchen, at the top of an old building. The other very large and unheated rooms would now be desirable 'apartments'.

Here we had our first real parties with cheap red wine, our first lovers, our first taste of the forbidden fruits.

But it wasn't a very long time before that was exchanged for husband, house and children.

Despite insistence on being different, inevitably some patterns were repeated. Some ingrained habits were hard to shake off and some for better, and some for worse, were passed on to the next generation.

Now these children in turn have grown and I find myself in a different place. The furniture is the same but the space is larger. There is a clearing and not just of the bits and pieces of three other lives. No, this is also a clearing of the mind. The time of parenting, in that sense, is over. For the first time I am carefree. This is an unaccustomed freedom. I watch as friends fill the empty nest with other fledglings, real or imagined, other wounded birds requiring their concern. I want to hold this space, walk around in it. It feels very different to that first freedom, which was a freedom from the restrictions of home, from a judging church, from a joyless faith.

This new freedom is not liberation from anything, but a freedom towards something, a recognition that this is the one and only life I have been given and it is mine to live fully, freely, hopefully, gratefully.

The burden of perfection

OH TO BE RELEASED FROM THE BURDEN OF BEAUTY.

The self-appointed guardians of our culture press on us counsels of perfection. Before our eyes so-called ugly ducklings are turned into swans – perfect plastic replicas of one another. They present themselves before us.

Oh to be freed from the insistence on the white
    gleaming smile,
the straightened nose, the unlined face, the
    perfectly groomed,
the polished and pruned.

Give me instead the wrinkles and warts.
Give me the age lines and laughter lines,
give me your lived-in sagging body,
give me your flawed and failing self.
And in your turn, forgive me,
all that I am not, all that I cannot be.

Grandmother saint

THOSE OF US NAMED ANNE OR MARY TEND TO BE OF A
certain age: the age of grandmothers. Their day is past
but may one day return as signs of nostalgia or sentiment
for the plain and simple rather than the exotic. The virtue
of the plain name is that it allows the bearer to fill it out
with meaning: Anne is a blank canvas; whereas a Daisy
might turn out to be most un-flower-like, and Scholastica
might want to be a model and not an academic; Kylie a
nuclear physicist rather than a pop star. I got irritated
if, as sometimes happened, I was called Mary instead of
Anne, or if the 'e' at the end of my name was omitted in
the spelling. Apart from that it was just my name. I didn't
think too much about the saint for whom I was called.

Then a few years ago I came across an unusual Christmas card: it was a scene from a fifteenth-century illuminated manuscript and it showed a 'holy family'; nothing unusual in that, but this was not Mary, Joseph and the child Jesus, with or without shepherds or kings. Instead it showed two women and a child. The large figure at the back was that of St Anne, and she was seated reading a book. Her eyes were on her reading, one hand holding the book while her other arm gently enfolded the young mother sitting beneath, and her hand was on the head of the child.

This was exciting: St Anne as a grandmother with Mary and with the child Jesus, and even better she was reading. She wasn't washing up, or making the tea. She was continuing to read, even as she offered her wise overseeing protection to the new mother and baby. After that I noted many images of St Anne teaching the virgin to read and later on an even more surprising medieval image of Mary post-partum, reading a book, while Joseph sat minding the child Jesus. I started to have rather more affection and interest in the iconography of the saint for whom I was named and now – as I delight in my small granddaughter's pleasure in books – even more do I treasure that image of Granny St Anne, who keeps one eye on her book and one hand on the head of the child.

Instructions for parents in the month of June

HAVING MOVED RECENTLY INTO GRANDMOTHER MODE I'M out of step with the parents of children sitting exams in the month of June. But oh it is all ahead of you, my dear daughter: you'll be the one crossing your fingers, untying knots in your tummy, trying to stay calm and trying to remember long forgotten prayers to long decommissioned saints when your own precious daughter comes to sit her leaving school exams – in sixteen years time. So here's the advice ... you'll remember all the things I did wrong and make your own mistakes in turn, but for now learn from this: when she comes in the door, wipe that anxious 'How did you get on?' look from your face. Instead place in front of her a plate of her favourite food; then busy yourself with your own affairs. When the tears come, let them – it will never be as bad as it seems – but don't do post-mortems, just do present un-tensing, and then do again as above, and if the food is taken away to eat while watching a silly soap (for you it was *Neighbours*), don't say, 'But you'd be better off going outside and getting some fresh air.'

Don't ask, 'Are you sure you've done enough revision?' Instead say, 'You'll be surprised how much comes back when you sit down with a pen in your hand.' (Except, of course, for your own daughter it may not be a pen at all, but for now it is.)

There may yet be a role for me. One June I watched an elegant grandmother (reminder: try to dress/behave like an elegant grandmother) sitting in a café, waiting for her granddaughters. They arrived wearing green school uniforms and looks of exam-weariness. She stood up and enfolded them in large hugs and ordered hot chocolates with marshmallows on top. You liked that too.

You see, we can do very little as parents, as grandparents: we can't live their lives for them; we can't sit their exams; we can't expect them to be like us; all that matters is for them to be themselves, and to like themselves. But we can offer hot chocolate and hugs, and sometimes that's enough.

Generations

MOTHER AND SON

A small boy sits next to his young mother playing with her long plait of hair. He clearly uses this to soothe himself and only reluctantly does he let go when they get off the tram. I am brought back to the early years of my own children and their attachment to things – often the most unlikely bits of cloth or ribbon which would turn to rags but which became essential comfort objects. In this case the child is attached to his mother's hair – what will he do when she leaves him? Will she have to cut off a piece of her long red plait and leave it on the pillow? Right now the child cannot imagine separation, but separate they will. This is what living in the world is about: separation, the leaving and the letting go. Sometimes it seems to me as if it is one long goodbye.

FATHER AND SON

The small boy is Asian, maybe Chinese, with a heavy shock of dark hair and a most wonderful smile. I catch his eye and stop to talk to him. Shy now, he turns away and hides his face. 'What a lovely child,' I exclaim, and the father smiles. 'His name is Vince,' he says. 'Vince' – this is most certainly not a Chinese name. This child was born here, one of the new Irish. He will grow up carrying his parents' culture in his blood and his adopted culture in his name. 'May you be always welcome here' is what I want to say, a blessing is what I want to give this child of promise, but the smile will have to do.

MOTHER AND DAUGHTER

'Oh Mum, how silly you are!' exclaims the young leggy teenager. She's going to be beautiful, no doubt about that. She is facing her mother – a mirror image in a different generation. Right now though, it is not likeness which preoccupies her but unlikeness.

Having been close, so close that not a hair's breath separated them, now she keeps her distance. She wants her space. She draws a circle around herself and for now her mother belongs outside. The mother, who once could do no wrong, now can do no right. This is painful. Some refuse to let go and pull the child back from the young woman that she is trying to become. Have trust. Let her go. Pass through those years and soon that circle will open again, perhaps through the birth of another daughter.

Fear and faith

WHEN THE CHRISTIAN CHURCHES CELEBRATE PENTECOST they celebrate a freedom from fear. The disciples are gathered in an upper room, according to Luke, and there they devote themselves to prayer. That is all well and good but there is a whole world outside that room. The rush of the pentecostal wind knocks the fear into them — and then out of them — and tongues as of fire rest on them, and they fling open the doors and go out to preach the good news. When fear drops away they find they have tongues to speak; they can be understood after all. They have not been given some exotic gift but the loosening of their tongues from the constricted knots in their throats. They are the same motley crew of fishermen and women followers struggling with faith and fear; now empowered by the spirit, they find their voice.

It is often assumed that the opposite of faith is un-faith or un-belief, but perhaps the opposite of faith is fear: fear of stepping out, fear of stepping on lines, fear of stepping on toes, fear of stepping into planes or trains; fear of saying the right thing, fear of saying the wrong thing; fear of birth, fear of death, and the crippling one, fear of failure.

These fears of all we can't control prevent us from falling: from falling into deep waters, from falling into mystery, from falling in love, from falling into faith ...

Vulnerable loving

Falling short, slipping through,
muddled and muddling
we make our way through the maze and haze of
  hurt and barbs
that shape us and mark us out as human travellers.
We are so capable of wounding one another;
we are so vulnerable ourselves.
And is it the fear of the latter that leads to the
  former?
Afraid of being caught out in our neediness and
  weakness
we hit out instead – warding off any possible
  arrows denting our armour.
We are fearful of being uncovered, discovered.
Yet without our cover being blown there is no
  hope of love;
for love is only possible where there is risk and
  trust.
A wise woman philosopher talks not of love
  affairs
but of life's affair being the work of love.*
She is consoling: we're bound to get it wrong all
  the time,
but we're bound to go on trying, for that is why we
  are here:
to learn, to practise the art of loving ...

again and again and again ... risking failure, risking
rejection, risking love.

* This 'wise woman philosopher' is Gillian Rose, and her *Love's Work*
(London: Chatto and Windus, 1995), 135

What mattered yesterday

What mattered yesterday was the conversation
    with the girl in the library
with her red-feathered earrings.
She was young and bright;
she came from Cork, or was it Galway?
A friendly place in any case.
What mattered yesterday
was an ordinary human exchange.
I had been struggling to come to the surface.
The surface was what I needed
not the muddied waters of the deep
where I had struggled for days
that seemed like weeks.
Not someone to ask
in concerned tones
'And how are you?'
No, just an ordinary chat
returning me to normality
to the surface of things

to the time before
things went black.
To the daily ordinariness
of the commonplace exchange.
Coming to the surface for air
I was helped by the girl in the library
oblivious to all that had happened
dispensing grace unbeknownst to herself
the girl with red-feathered earrings.

San Antonio

ON A STUDY TOUR TO PADUA OUR GUIDE, AN ARCHITECTURAL historian, took us around the wonderful basilica of San Antonio. He pointed to its architectural highlights, its ancient cloisters, its frescoed chapels. Then as we were about to finish, he added: 'Now go and join the pilgrims who are here to visit the relics [a piece of the tongue of St Anthony] and to touch his tomb.' I was taken aback: visiting relics is not part of my usual faith practice.

Then a comment from another member of the group stopped me in my somewhat arrogant tracks: 'It's like a constant cycle of prayer as you walk in the footsteps of the pilgrims.' I joined the group at the side chapel, pleased that the queue wasn't long and that soon I would be at lunch. I found myself next to an Italian family all in their Sunday best: grandparents pushing a double-buggy with twin baby boys, two little girls in navy and white dresses walking alongside, a small boy in his smart suit. As we approached the tomb the young father lifted one of the sleeping babies out of his pushchair and carried him the last few paces. He turned to me as if apologising for the delay as he settled his child. My rudimentary grasp of Italian was sufficient to understand what he was saying: 'It is important I lift him up – *Si chiama Antonio*, he is called Anthony.' And with that he took his child's tiny fingers and laid them on the tomb. I was standing next to him, and instinctively placed my hand on the child's head, 'the *little* blessed Antonio'. I then placed my own hand on the tomb.

The story I told at lunch was very different to the one I had anticipated telling. I had started the tour to the tomb as a curious tourist but had completed it as a praying pilgrim. Later I spoke to our guide and told him the story and was curious about his insistence that we do this bit also. 'Well,' he said, 'I've been trying to show you that if you want to understand buildings you must walk through the spaces. I expect it is similar with tombs and relics – you must walk with pilgrims to understand the pilgrimage.'

Learning by heart

LEARNING BY HEART IS A MUCH-MALIGNED PRACTICE. IT is now seen as largely redundant, belonging to less enlightened schooldays. I can remember the teacher who, when asked why we should learn yet another poem by heart, told us that one day we might go blind. We were as little persuaded by that argument as we were by the admonition to 'eat up your dinner; there are children starving' (to which the response could only be, 'Well, let them have mine').

I'm not sure either that there was too much heart in that rote learning, where missing a beat often meant getting a beating.

Choosing to remember and learn a loved piece of poetry or music is quite a different matter. Knowing something by heart gives it both the familiarity and the surprise of the loved person or thing. We remember it and it remembers us. Anyone who has ever had the experience of reading to a small child knows that they demand to hear the same story over and over again, apparently instinctively recognising that stories shape experience and that learning by heart helps them to inhabit this strange world.

Now at this midlife stage I recognise that I have acquired 'habits of the heart'. I see my mother's gestures in mine as I take down a favourite poem and read it to my grandchildren and hope that it will be embedded in their imaginations as it was in mine.

Imagination at play

I WAS JUST DOZING OFF ON THE TRAIN ON MY WAY HOME FROM a busy day when I overheard snippets of a conversation.

> SMALL CHILD: 'Granddad, did you ever go up in a rocket?'

> *I didn't catch the reply, but presume it was in the*
> *negative. Pause.*
> SMALL CHILD: 'Did any of our family ever go up in
> a rocket?'
> *Granddad, perhaps looking over his paper, shakes his*
> *head again.*
> SMALL CHILD *with one last hope:* 'What about Aunt
> Betsy? Did she ever go up in a rocket?'

I had been smiling from the beginning of the conversation but now I was suppressing my laughter at the thought of Aunt Betsy in a rocket. I saw her in high heels, and wearing a hat, dressed as if for a wedding or a christening, and hopping into a rocket with her small grandnephew cheering her on. I was reminded of a contemporary rendering of a medieval mystery play where, so I'm told, they put a little old lady sporting a straw hat in a rocket, to portray the Assumption of Mary.

I thought of what a wonderful gift the imagination is and also of how small children are infinitely inquisitive. 'Why?' they ask and continue asking until the wearied parent can take no more, 'Just because ...' or until one day someone responds, 'Don't be stupid'. And the child whose dreams had been soaring has her wings cut and drops to earth and learns to mimic acceptable forms of fantasy and joins her brother absorbed in the latest computer game.

It so happened that the first reading the following Sunday (Trinity Sunday) was that piece from Proverbs (8:22-31): 'I was by his side, like a craftsperson [or a little child] ... ever at play ... at play everywhere in the world ...

delighting in the human race.' I found myself thinking of how little we look at 'play' as something emanating from the Divine. We feel righteous when we work, somewhat guilty when we daydream, and 'play' is only for children. At a certain age we stop playing; we no longer 'go out to play'. The slight uncertainty in the text as to whether the word used is 'artisan' or 'little child' is rather pleasing, as artists are those who continue 'to play'. Their curiosity about the world has not been dulled and their capacity to make ludicrous – that is utterly playful – connections remains intact. They surprise us. They delight us.

The small boy who could imagine that Aunt Betsy might, even *might have* gone up in a rocket, will grow up to be an inventor or an artist, a poet or a dreamer until, unless, someone pulls him down to earth, rubs his nose in the dust, or simply turns on the television.

The leap of poetry and the leap of faith

AMERICAN POET DENISE LEVERTOV SPEAKS TO MY condition of ambivalence. She writes of doubt and faith and the dark places of unbelief, and composes a poem called 'Mass for the Day of St Thomas Didymus' (Doubting Thomas), which includes a Credo with the lines, 'I believe and interrupt my belief with doubt, I doubt and interrupt my doubt with belief.' She observes that the experience of writing the poem became a kind of conversion, a practice of faith.

The poet knows the torment of relentless questioning, the almost helpless rage against the self-destructive nature of our species and yet the thread that draws us on. For her there is a parallel between the journey of imagination and the journey of faith. She talks about living with 'a door of one's life open to the transcendent, the numinous'. She refers to an almost insistent sense of awe and gratitude in her own life's experience and so makes a decision to act as if she did believe: to practise faith by praying, by participating in the rituals of the Church – a suspension of disbelief one might call it.

There is a parallel in the writing process. Both require the leap into the unknown, a plunging into the darkness, a refusal to block out the shadows or numb the pain. She calls it 'swimming through waters of unknown depth' and comments that the very act of embracing the darkness or the pain of diving into those deep waters becomes itself the process of conversion, of healing. Poets don't deal in certainties; they play with ambiguity, with paradox, sifting through the confusion of what it is to be human. They nurture the imagination, expanding the little world we construct and control because we fear the unknown and the strange.

Poetry is not a distraction from life but close attention to it. Through the imagination we learn to inhabit both pain and joy at a more intense level; we discover ourselves as destroyers and creators. And it is just possible that we begin to learn and practise compassion until the wings, trailing in the dust, lift, and 'dull stones again fulfil their glowing destinies'.*

—⊰✦⊱—

* Quotes from essays 'Work that Enfaiths' and 'A Poet's View' in *New and Selected Essays* (New York: New Directions, 1992), 249–50 and 241 respectively. Line from 'Mass for the Day of St Thomas Didymus' from *New and Selected Poems* (Tarset: Bloodaxe Books, 2003), 130. Line from 'The Tide' from *'The Stream and the Sapphire': Selected Poems on Religious Themes* (New York: New Directions, 1997), 25

Annunciations

'WHAT DO YOU THINK THOSE HANDS ARE SAYING?' ASKS MY husband, as we stand in front of a Botticelli annunciation in the Uffizi gallery in Florence. The hand of the angel is raised in blessing, in greeting, but Mary's hands gesture away from her body, 'No, no,' she seems to say, 'this is too much', or perhaps she is simply asking for time. In a Duccio annunciation the hands are raised as if in horror, 'What is this? You can't mean me!' I'm told there is an annunciation in Bruges where Mary is depicted with a nosebleed brought on by the shock at the change in atmosphere. I certainly know another painting where a cat arches its back at the sight of the visitor.

There is a very different scene in the Dominican cloister of San Marco in Florence. Fra Angelico depicts his Madonna with hands folded across her breast, yet what might be read as passivity becomes a moment of harmony between messenger and recipient, as his angel mirrors that same gesture. It becomes a moment of waiting, of mystical stillness.

A young Japanese woman is the only other visitor on the cold February morning. She hesitates and then asks, 'Please can you tell me why this picture is so special? I like it very much.'

We look at it together, the young woman from the East, the older woman from the West. Do we share any of the same experience?

I try to tell her why it captivates me. I talk about the separate spaces between the virgin and the angel, the sense of stillness and the space that draws you in so that you, the onlooker, become part of this moment of invitation, this threshold moment of call and response. I want to tell her that this is a prayer that happens to be a painting. Does this mean anything? I don't know.

She listens and nods vigorously. Can one explain a thing of beauty? Is it about strokes of the brush, choice of colour? Is the immediacy of the fresco, the paint on fresh plaster, what gives this its fragile and numinous quality?

It is clear that she too has sensed that this is something more than a painting in a gallery. This is a sacred object, this is a sacred space, and so is our encounter.

Martha's tasks

BECAUSE OF A SHORT STORY IN LUKE'S GOSPEL ABOUT Martha and Mary, which tells of Mary sitting at Jesus' feet and listening, women have been told that women's work is not 'the better part'. Because of a long history of men interpreting the scriptures for women, women have believed that Martha was in the kitchen.

I love the kitchen, it's a great place to be, but only if you choose it, not if you're confined there.

I've read that story again and the surprising thing is that nowhere does it actually say that Martha is in the kitchen. It was just assumed. What else would a woman be busy about? Where else would she be?

Well, once we stop assuming that a woman's place is only in the kitchen, I can think of many things that Martha might have been doing, that she might do.

She might have been preparing a sermon; she might have been composing some music; she might have been instructing the disciples; she might have been writing a poem or a gospel ...

THE BREAD OF OUR MOTHERS

The bread of our mothers has nurtured many of us, perhaps rather more than 'the faith of our fathers'. Bread making and breaking in various forms shape both domestic and religious lives. These are practices into which we have been initiated and which in turn we pass on, perhaps in changed forms, but with the common core of sustaining and celebrating life. As human creatures we need food, we need drink and we need picnics and parties too. The exchange of hospitality is the natural outreach from this centre. Yet this too is tinged with ambiguity, and some of the following pieces explore the vulnerabilities of guests and hosts in their exchanges.

The bread of our mothers

I HAVE THE BOWL, A KIND OF MUSTARD YELLOW OUTSIDE with a diamond pattern etched into it, white inside aged with cracks. I have the wooden spoon, or one of its kind.

I have the recipe, although she didn't use one – a handful of this, a scoop of that.

Mix the flour – wholemeal with a dash of white for lightness – a pinch of salt, two teaspoons of bread soda, well mixed so there's no bitterness. Add enough buttermilk to make a soft dough. Knead lightly. My buttermilk comes from a plastic bottle. Hers came from a blue and white striped jug.

Did the milkman not come and pour buttermilk straight from an urn into her jug as she held it out on the doorstep? And did she not then keep a bit back as a starter for the next lot that sat on the counter until just right, thick and yellow, ready to make good bread? It all depends on the buttermilk, its readiness, its level of sweet sourness.

She mixes her bread quickly and deftly shapes it with her large hands. Her hands are dusty with flour and her face reddened from the heat of the oven. Her touch is light and the bread rounds under her hands as she swiftly marks it with a cross before placing it in the oven.

Did that help it to cook evenly? Or was the crossing of the bread a sign from an older tradition that marked all doings with a prayer? In either case my mother gave us 'our daily bread', and when we left home it was what we missed.

I tried to make her bread but failed. So now I follow a different recipe. Mine gets spooned into a tin and covered with seeds – good for the health, I'm sure, but there's no shaping of the round loaf, no marking with a cross and yet ...

Catechesis in the kitchen

THE FOUR FRIENDS HADN'T MET FOR A LONG TIME. THERE was a slight awkwardness between them. How do you begin again? Catching up with events of the missing years could become as trivial as the updates on a CV, as artificial as the highlights of the Christmas round robin. It is always the gaps that are more interesting.

A walk helps, and then the four prepare a meal together. It is in the peeling of the roots, the chopping of the vegetables, the stirring of the soup that the talk really begins to flow again.

'This is what I used to do with my confirmation classes,' our host, a Lutheran woman pastor, explains. 'We had kitchen catechesis. The boys in particular loved it. With their fingers stained red from beetroot I'd slip in some comment about redemption; with their eyes tearing up from the cutting of the onions I'd hear about the tough stuff in their lives; with their heads bent in concentration on the chopping of white cabbage, I'd talk about prayer.'

Then of course they would sit and eat, as we did also. The mystery of the Trinity, a communion in love, was explored in the making of borscht, a Russian vegetable soup, velvety and sweet to taste, served with sour cream.

A last supper

WE HAD A PARTY TWO DAYS BEFORE MY FATHER DIED. WE didn't know then that he was about to die, although we knew that his time was limited. He had come out of hospital for the occasion – our son's eighteenth birthday as it happened.

It was a beautiful day, the sun shone. A typical gathering: siblings argued; we exchanged stories; grandchildren played in the garden. Everyone dropped in and out to chat with my father, who was surprisingly cheerful and made his usual cryptic comments, 'Ah, real food at last', when a granddaughter, who had flown home from Italy to surprise him, brought him his lunch. When he had enough of food and conversation, he left – that too was true to form, he was not a party man. Then two days later he died suddenly. The Sunday lunch had become a Last Supper and we went over every detail remembering what he said, regretting what we didn't say.

The Eucharist celebrated at his funeral gathered up the crumbs from that party and made sense of them and of all our eating and drinking, our mourning and laughing.

Table-fellowship

EATING AND DRINKING IS WHAT WE DO – NOT JUST TO sustain life but also to celebrate it. We rejoice in company: companions are – quite literally – those with whom we break bread (the word coming from the Latin *com,* 'with', and *panis*, 'bread'). Table-fellowship in kitchens and dining rooms, canteens and coffee shops takes us out of our isolation into communion. We gather and eat together in celebration, at births, at marriages, at deaths, and every occasion in between.

Standing around at drinks parties doesn't do it. We need to put our feet under the table.

We share food and stories, memories and hopes. To be at the table together is no guarantee of domestic harmony; it may in fact be the very place where most arguments happen. However, sharing food, breaking bread together, suggests that we are made, not simply to consume in order to survive, but that in order to thrive we need communion.

If this were not the case, then the Sunday ritual breaking of bread would make no sense. The truth is that for many it is meaningless, either because they no longer break bread together in their own homes, or because what goes on at those rituals in no way resembles their own bread-breaking.

Either way the connection is lost.

Boundary-making

THE SMALL BOY WAS HAULED BACK BY HIS MOTHER FROM gate-crashing (or more accurately fence-jumping) a neighbouring house where there was a children's party. 'But,' he wailed, 'they have a bouncing castle, and bouncing castles are for all kids!' His mother tries to explain the principle of exclusion and the child learns about life's injustices. 'When we have a party all the kids can come,' he insists.

All groups define themselves as much by those they exclude as those they include. Our comfort zones determine our guest lists.

The boundaries we erect to mark out our territories have become more visible in our society with the presence of gated estates. It is not simply that the houses are not open, but you need permission even to go down the road. And there is no chance of the child straying into the path of the elderly neighbours who live outside the gates, or offering to carry their bags, as we used to do as children, with the sure promise of a chocolate biscuit or a boiled sweet. 'Wonderful to know they are safe,' say the mothers, whose children sit with glazed eyes in front of the television, as the neat patch of communal grass, on which in any case they are not permitted to play, remains untouched. And so the child learns that 'people like us' live here, and even if the gates are opened the barriers are now internalised.

And some miles away there is another estate that this child will also never enter and it too is barred, but in this case by burnt-out cars and fear of joyriders.

Both places are 'no-go' areas.

Hospitality and sneezes

OUR VISITORS HAD ARRIVED TO SPEND A HOLIDAY WITH US in a cottage in the West of Ireland. By Sunday I was beginning to feel edgy – only three days into their stay. We are not used to sharing this space. We have become accustomed in recent years to our privacy and peace here and it is easy to be reclusive in the remoteness of the Connemara landscape. I was discovering the limitations of my hospitality, the cracks where theories of welcome meet practices of welcoming. Our guests were considerate and gracious; the problem was with the host. So I took myself and my petty irritations to the small chapel of the Benedictine Abbey near where we were staying.

I was buying myself some peace, leaving the sleeping guests. I was expecting some gentle singing and a calm atmosphere, but I hadn't reckoned with the readings. They were all on the theme of hospitality. I listened to the story of Elisha the prophet visiting the woman of Shumen who decides to build him a small apartment – an upper room where he can rest when he passes through. The theme of the Gospel too was 'welcoming the stranger'.

I wanted to put my hand up and say, 'Alright, alright, guilty as charged'. At the end of that first story when the prophet raises the woman's son to life, the child sneezes. As I listened to the homily and the elderly monk referred to this moment, I tried unsuccessfully to suppress a sneeze. (Is there not a folk tradition about sneezing being a way of letting the devil out? Hence the 'bless you' which follows.) In any case I felt blessed: having entered scowling, I left the chapel smiling, wanting to share the joke. On the return journey I reflected on how the problem was not that I hadn't been doing enough, but that I'd been trying too hard. I needed to stop and let go and let be instead of blocking the flow of grace. I walked into the cottage and smelt the coffee. 'How was church?' they asked. 'Great!' I replied, 'I wish you'd been there, too', and I meant it.

The duties of guests — particularly in the morning

HOSPITALITY, ACCORDING TO MY DICTIONARY, CONCERNS the friendly welcome and entertainment of guests. It is a particular practice or charism of the Benedictine Order who are instructed to receive all who come as if they were receiving Christ himself. The role of Guest Master is an important one in the Order, providing this welcome, offering a quiet, unobtrusive presence.

However, some guests try even the patience of a monk. There is a story told about a certain Benedictine Guest Master who, when recognising a familiar figure making his way up the drive, was heard to mutter, 'O Christ, not you again!'

But surely guests have their responsibilities too. There is a word for that, which could do with reviving: *hospitage,* pertaining to the behaviour expected of guests. In monasteries this might mean respecting the boundaries of places and persons. The restrictions of the cloister begin to make sense. It helps to delineate spaces for encounter, and spaces for silence, spaces for engagement, and spaces for withdrawal. In this age of chat shows and so-called 'reality' TV, counter-cultural good practice might require one to hold back rather than pour out every undigested thought, every anguish of the soul.

House guests should show a similar respect for boundaries, particularly at breakfast time, when hosts should be left alone with their cornflakes to ease their way into the first smile of the day. On no account should cheery conversation be offered or questions asked about politics or culture. The quality of hospitality can be strained, especially early in the morning.

Hostility and hospitality

SOMETIMES YOU DISCOVER SOMETHING THAT OPENS UP A space where the imagination is teased into fresh explorations of once familiar territory. Learning about the original meaning of the words 'guest' and 'host' became one such moment for me. I learn that they are intimately connected, sharing similar roots: host and guest stand at the same threshold linked by reciprocal fear; host and guest hover at the same threshold invited to mutual trust.

Both words can be traced back to the same Latin word *hostis,* meaning stranger or enemy. The stranger is always other and different; such difference comes as threat or gift. Thus the word travels along one trajectory, picking up generous impulses of welcome, kindness, friendship, hospitality.

Along the other path the word picks up resentment, fear, anger, threat, hostility.

On both routes there are the strangers, by definition displaced, walking the road in fear and trembling, wondering what their reception will be.

> What language are they speaking?
> What do these gestures mean?
> Are these strangers plotting to harm us?
> Are they bearing gifts ... or guns?
> Or are they simply asking for directions, or for
>   bread?

Hostility jostles with hospitality as the stranger waits to be rejected as enemy, or to be received as guest.

Vulnerable strangers

IN THE ANCIENT WORLD A HOSPICE WAS A HOUSE FOR THE entertainment of strangers, a hospital a house for travellers. Hospitality was the art of welcoming the stranger.

A hospice is now a home for the care of the terminally ill, a place of comfort for the dying. A hospital is an institution for the treatment of the sick. Hospitality is the art of welcoming the stranger.

The common denominator between meanings old and new is in 'vulnerability'. Vulnerable: capable of being physically or emotionally wounded. The stranger is vulnerable before the host: unsure as to how she will be received, awkward about customs with cutlery or dress.

Travellers and strangers originally looked to the hospice, the hospital, the hostel to provide them with comfort and courtesy as they journeyed.

Today patients wait on hospital trolleys in A&E departments. They too are vulnerable, incapable of lifting head or raising voice; they are certainly physically, and probably emotionally, wounded also.

Of the original hospital as a place of welcome for the stranger, the place of repose, even of entertainment, of that they know little, they find few connections, few resonances.

They simply want a bed.

Hosts, hostages and hope

ON THE DARKEST SHADOW SIDE OF HOSPITALITY WE FIND 'hostage taking'. It is the very antithesis of that gracious act: the host brings choice food and drink for the guests, the hostage taker throws a lump of dry bread into the cell. The host offers water to wash dusty hands or feet, the hostage taker refuses these basic needs. The host generously offers their space, the hostage taker confines the captive. The host engages in conversation, the hostage taker refuses communication. The host greets with an embrace, the hostage taker with a beating. The door of the host's house is open for coming and going. The hostage taker bars the door and chains the prisoner.

And in between the generous impulses of hospitality and the violent impulses of hostage taking there are the mundane exercises of social exchange – planned giving and planned receiving, which characterise most of our dealings with one another.

Reports of violence and terror on the one hand and narratives of trust and compassion on the other, teach us that there are heights and depths of the human heart unfamiliar and sometimes alien to us, some of which lead us to despair of this condition which we share, and others of which inspire us and give us hope.

The kindness of strangers

RICHARD DAWKINS AND HIS ILK DON'T LIKE IT. THEY TALK about the selfish gene. They are puzzled by random acts of kindness. Are such acts genetically predisposed in human beings? Or have they evolved with society? Well, neither sociology nor biology is of much concern to the woman standing by the side of the road with a burst tyre.

All she knows is that as soon as the car shuddered to a halt and she got out to see the damage, a young man was standing there offering help. She had already driven two hours in stormy weather and all she wanted was home.

Where did he come from, the red-headed stranger? She didn't know.

He steered the car to safety, and finding the spare wheel, jacked the car up and replaced it.

Oh, and did I mention that he went to his house nearby for the hammer needed to knock off the damaged tyre? And that all this time it was raining. She wondered how she should thank him. She asked what she might do. He wanted nothing, saying simply that perhaps someone would look after his family in a similar manner one day if they should ever need it.

The sociologists can continue their research, the biologists can conduct their experiments, but there is a grace that flows from 'the kindness of strangers' that is not measurable by any such means.

It renews our trust. It restores our hope. It takes us home.

Making room

THEY STOOD OUTSIDE THE CHURCH ON CHRISTMAS morning: the young Indian couple with their small son. We had never seen them there before. The parents smiled shyly and introduced themselves. As we talked I asked what their plans were for the day. 'We might go into the city,' they answered. I had this vision of the empty streets of the town, so different from the buzz and excitement of Christmas Eve. 'Oh, you mustn't do that,' I found myself saying, 'why don't you come to our house?'

I explained that at Christmas time there was always plenty of food and there was always room. They exchanged quiet words. 'If you are sure,' said the father, 'we would be happy to come.' 'Of course,' I replied, and looked to our children who nodded in agreement, and then called my husband over, saying, 'Meet our guests from Mysore, in India – they're coming to us for Christmas dinner.' 'That's great!' he replied.

I decided to walk with the Indian family and let the others go ahead by car, to give everyone a short space to adjust, and as I did the small boy put his hand into mine, and I knew everything would be alright.

When we got home our son was in the kitchen. After some warming drinks he invited our guests to join him chopping and peeling and adding some spices to the roast vegetables so that the food would not be too bland for them. In this space the shyness eased with the communal task of preparation. Our enchanted daughters meanwhile happily entertained the small boy. When the doorbell rang and friends arrived for Christmas drinks, he looked up and waved a greeting, as if he was already 'at home'.

When we took our places at the long table now set for ten, the small boy whispered something to his mother, pointing to my husband. 'He has just said "Grandfather" in Hindi,' she explained. We were honoured. We had thought we were bringing these people into our family, but they were also bringing us into theirs.

In the days that followed all of our adult children agreed that this was probably the best Christmas since their childhood. What we will remember always is how this family, arriving as strangers, departing as guests, became gift and grace for us.

Bread-making

TAKE SOME YEAST, FRESH IF YOU CAN GET IT, WITH ITS pungent smell and looking like a block of putty. Mix it with some warmed milk and water, blood-heat is good. Add some honey for sweetening.

You'll soon see a frothy head – like a good pint of a well-known brew. Mix this with some measures of flour, strong for bread making; throw in a pinch of salt.

As it comes together, turn out and knead well. You must use your hands. There are machines of course, but they give you neither the sensuous feel of the bread becoming soft and round under your hands nor an outlet for frustration as you pummel the bread. Your anger will die and your bread will rise.

You can, indeed you should, offer a piece of the dough to the small, or not so small, child who stands watching you. Handling this dough will do it no harm, and will do them much good.

'Now for the magic part,' you tell them, 'we will wait for the dough to rise.' Cover it gently with a cloth and go away and do something else. You'll get two hours in the garden or at your desk if you're lucky, two hours housework if you're not.

When you return, the dough will have risen to meet the cloth and even the child's small ball will have become a balloon.

Punch it down and release the air.

Shape it now: take three strands and plait them just like the plaits you used to admire in Mary D's hair in primary school. Join the ends to make a circle. Let it rise again. (The child will make a snake or a monster. Raisins are good for eyes.) Brush with egg yolk or milk. Add some poppy seeds if you like. Place in a hot oven. Remove the risen golden wreath of bread some thirty minutes later. It won't be perfect – who wants perfect? But it will be wonderful. Set it upon the table and call whoever is around to come and smell, to break and eat. (The child will insist on giving you a crumb of the monster, and you will taste it and it too will be good.)

Bread-breaking

They knew him in the breaking of the bread.
—Luke 24

OF THE FOUR RESURRECTION NARRATIVES THIS IS THE ONE that makes most sense to me. Maybe I am too earth-bound for angel messengers and empty tombs, sudden appearances through locked doors. This, however, is a story that follows the contours of human experience, the overwhelming grief and loss that blinds the travellers as they journey away from Jerusalem, according to Luke.

In their confusion and despair they fail to recognise the stranger with whom they walk. Locked into the past of their grief they are not open to present hope. They tell their story of dreams unravelled, of the commonplace crucifixion of an uncommon man for whom their hopes had been so high.

He listens, this pilgrim stranger, takes up their tale and tells it back to them, shaping a different story out of the same elements, as only a graced storyteller can. However, words alone will not assuage their sorrow, nor roll back the stone from hearts hardened almost to despair, hearts defended against more pain.

Yet there is a chink of light, some glimpse of hope, because they lift their eyes from the ground long enough to see the other and invite him to share their lodging.

There is a painting by the Sienese painter Duccio that shows the two travellers turning to invite the as yet unrecognised companion into the lodging place. The door is closed and looks like the entrance to a tomb, but in this case the final unlocking will come, not through any more words or wondrous deeds but when the pilgrim stranger takes some bread, blesses it, breaks it and gives it to them.

The scales lift from their eyes, and as they see with that 'Ah!' of recognition, he disappears from their sight.

But they continue to remember him in the breaking of the bread.

Waiting for dolphins and watching for geese

For a time I was obsessed by the desire to see dolphins. This longing seemed to reflect a kind of restlessness that keeps our desire and passion for living keen and sharp and ensures that we are never fully satisfied. One would imagine then that a fulfilment of this wish would end that 'searching' but it doesn't. I won't anticipate the piece here but simply say that a sighting evokes not relief that the desire is fulfilled, but a momentary glimpse of joy and an urge to praise. My companion obsession was with Brent geese and in this case I noted that it was something about their migratory journeys with which I identified, and so I have woven in some other tales of journeys. The nature pieces are included less as observations on the natural world but more because of what they evoke and their common threads with the other pieces in this collection, with similar tones of attention to the present moment and alertness to ruptures of grace.

Waiting for dolphins

A VISITOR'S BOOK IS KEPT AND IT HAS BECOME THE CUSTOM to note the sights and sounds of nature, and so you might read: 'A storm blew up and the spray reached the windows'; 'We heard a curlew'; 'The wrens are building a nest under the eaves', and so on. And it seems that every time we visit, someone has recorded a sighting of dolphins in the bay.

I am filled with envy. When we are there I scan the bay with the field glasses, eager at every lift of a wave or ripple in the water. I look for, and imagine, that magical sight of the graceful curved body, the fins lifting out of the water.

But I have not seen the dolphins.

This year was the worst – one glorious morning after a still, clear night we met fishermen at the harbour who related that the previous evening they had turned off the engines to watch a pair of dolphins play around the boat. I had seen the boat in the distance but not the dolphins. Later I related the incident to friends who live in the area. 'They are there alright. You have to learn to see them.'

The dolphins have become for me like an image of grace – it cannot be grasped, it can only be received, and one day the scales will fall from my eyes and I will see clearly, and a gasp of delight will announce the presence of the dolphins.

Attention

FROM EARLY SPRING I START TO THINK ABOUT GOING WEST to Connemara. I need that place. It restores my soul. Once there I feel myself slowly uncurling from the taut knot city life has wound me into.

It takes a while though before I can see or hear. Away from the almost incessant noises of the city – from traffic to builder's drills, from mobile phones to the relentless beat of shopping centre music – I have to learn again to attend. I don't want to drive. I want no scenic tours through the landscape, no matter how beautiful. I want to walk, and then later I will cycle. But first I want to walk. I feel the rain on my face and then warmth as sun breaks through the clouds, and then only slowly do I begin to see again. I make my way across the rocks to the lighthouse.

At first the colours are blurred: grey of rock, blue of sea, green of grass. Slowly, slowly my eyes pick up the miniature flowers in the crevices of the rocks; the vague whiteness reveals itself as a sea of bog cotton. I crouch down very closely and gaze at it waving gently in the breeze. I pause by a rock pool and peer into its mysterious depths. Nothing there, I think, and then a flicker as a fish darts into the side and then a shadow moves and is a crab.

Now I begin to hear. I turn my head to pick up the sound of the stonechats. I lie on the grass and listen to the crickets. I sit on a rock and watch as the sea laps in. I dip my feet in the water and feel the icy coldness.

Later I will come down again to the rocks, and if the sky is clear I will see the sun setting over the water. I will watch as the light passes over it, as the sea ripples like shot silk.

Then I will turn and go back up and into the cottage, deserted at the time of the famine and now lovingly brought to life again. I will stop at the door and look at the stone for grinding corn, broken when those who had no corn were forced to leave. Now the two pieces are carefully placed together again but the break between them holds the memory. I will remember those who once lived there and those who live here now and who so graciously share it with others. I call down blessings on all of them.

Trusting the waters

I THINK THE SEA MUST BE IN MY BLOOD. MY FATHER LOVED the sea, and until shortly before he became ill and died at the age of eighty-two he had been swimming regularly all year round.

Less of a swimmer than a walker by the sea, I had just dipped my toes into the cold waters of the Atlantic in June and now I'm back in mid-September. The sea should be warmer after that rarest of things here, a good summer. Following a misty day the skies are just beginning to lift a little now, and refusing to test the waters this time I run straight into the sea. Within minutes I come up laughing. I've never experienced such balmy waters here. For ten days this becomes the evening ritual, the evening song. Swimming in that shimmering light is magical. You can feel the warmth of the late sun on your body as you are gently lifted up and over the waves. You swim towards the light and your body seems to glow with it. Sometimes the sea is silver, sometimes rippled blue and green, always changing.

One evening a walker dressed warmly in his woollen sweater passes by and looks in astonishment at this middle-aged mermaid emerging from the water. 'What's it like?' he asks. 'Wonderful,' I reply, and can see that he doesn't believe me. I remember a young woman I met in Australia who said that surfing the waves was the closest that she'd ever get to an experience of God. For me it is the magic of the buoyancy, the sense of being held. I think that at this stage of my life I'm finally learning to trust. 'Don't fight it,' my father advised, teaching me to swim many moons ago. I'm sensible though of the dangers of the sea and happy to have my land companion keeping watch and waiting for me with a towel. I come out, do a little dance along the beach, and with my toe draw a circle and write 'Alleluia!'

Then we sit and watch the setting sun and wait until the waves wash over and swallow my words, taking them back out to sea.

Lettergesh in September

IT IS A MISTY MORNING. YOU CAN ONLY JUST MAKE OUT the islands across the sea. The air is still, unlike yesterday when wild winds came from the south-west, and when we went to walk the beach we returned home with our hair and clothes full of sand and we needed to shake down and shower off.

It is September, that time when only the stragglers of holidaymakers are left. Across the road from the house – once the schoolmaster's residence – the children have gone back to school and the place returns to its usual rhythms and we try to fall in with them. We pick blackberries and make some jam, filling old beetroot jars collected by Mikey next door. Later we will bring him a pot of the jam.

We were spoiled one year when there was an Indian summer and Connemara was more beautiful than we had ever seen it. The September light was magical with the colours just beginning to change, the gorse burnished by the sun. We try not to have expectations; however, it will be fine with us. It is as if we have a pact here. We keep coming, like old lovers, accepting this place for better or worse, in good weather and bad and trusting that the grey mists will eventually break through and reveal those wondrous mountains, that crop of islands and the sea, the sea.

Winter in Errislannan

'THE MICE MAY HAVE MOVED IN,' WARNS THE OWNER, BUT we see no sign. However the windows are flecked white with bird droppings and with salt spray carried up by the winds from the sea below. A pair of blue tits feed from peanuts in a remarkably domestic scene, considering the barren landscape. Robins visit and we just glimpse the tiny wren before she disappears in a flash of her upturned tail. A mad blackbird startles us by beating its wings on the windowpane as if to remind us that we are the intruders here. The fuchsia bushes outside are bare and ugly shorn with spikes, like Mohican haircuts, giving not even a hint of the rich green and red they will carry later in the year.

As I look out, the late rising winter sun is breaking through clouds and catching and colouring everything it touches. One distant hill has been caught and transfigured by golden light. It has its brief moment of glory before the light fades from it, and the sun passes to paint another rock or island, and the hill fades to that familiar Paul Henry blue. From the window we watch seabirds somersaulting as they dive for fish, and waves rising up around distant rocks and spilling down like whales spouting water. We half long for a storm like the one that sent enormous clumps of seaweed and other detritus over the harbour wall. Later we walk along an even wilder shore with waves lashing against the rocks and water being sucked in through a blowhole. We see the bay empty of its summer surfers and experience something of that sense of awe that anyone living close to the sea must feel. It is both wonderful and terrifying.

In this isolated cottage at the end of a peninsula on the far west coast, we are insulated against wind and storm, and for some days are content until the urge for company other than our own sends us home again.

Stars

ONE OF THE SAD THINGS ABOUT CITY LIFE IS THE ABSENCE of the dark. This may seem a strange thing to say, particularly in the grey days of January. But what I am talking about is the true dark of the night which is dulled by the omnipresence of lights, which, except on the clearest of nights, blot out the stars.

Away from the city in a different landscape it is another story. Here it is not the occasional star, twinkling in the sky, as the childhood rhyme has it, but an infinity of stars – you stand under the great dome of the sky and look up to a sparkling brightness and sense your place in the scale of things.

In the winter the sky glitters and the ground frosts over and you are grateful to go back inside to firelight and candlelight. In late summer you walk home under a starlit sky, maybe even sit outside and, if you are lucky, see some shooting stars.

You begin to understand how other peoples in other times might have been guided by the stars as they searched the sky for signs and portents.

Pity the child who has been brought to see the Christmas lights but has never stood still and gazed at the stars. Pity the young person for whom stargazing has nothing to do with the night sky or who thinks of star signs and horoscopes rather than the Plough or the Milky Way. Pity those who plod home under the artificial orange of a neon-lit sky and can never feel that draw to look up and beyond, whose imaginations cannot be stirred by the awesome thought that we are created from the ashes of dead stars.

The bog road

WE ARRIVED IN HEAVY RAIN AND MIST AND COULD SEE nothing and do little, but each day gradually brightened. And then one night the sky glittered with stars promising cold but clear days to follow. The next day dawned crisply bright and beautiful, a frost covering the ground and the stalks of the reeds painted white. The winter-rusted bracken which the previous day had glowed wine-red in the late sun was now a tracery of silver.

I decide to walk the bog road. To my left are the mountains, the Twelve Bens of Connemara, and on both sides there is the bog and the lakes. On this first morning of the New Year there is not a cloud in the sky. The sun catches shards of ice looking like pieces of glass as they lie scattered where a passing car has disturbed a frozen pothole. There is an extraordinary stillness, to which, every so often, like Elijah, I have to stop and listen.

For company I have only the sheep, who gaze in a desultory manner before they teeter across the road in their opaque black tights. One solitary cyclist, an elderly man in brown corduroy trousers held by bicycle clips, passes by and we exchange greetings, or rather praises – 'Beautiful day!' we call out to one another. And in a surreal moment an empty hearse speeds by, and I am distracted by the thought of someone, somewhere, breathing out their last, as I breathe in the glories of the day.

As I walk I feel that sense of rhythm that you get when the road is long and stretches ahead of you, but you have no purpose other than the walk and its pleasure. 'What were you thinking about?' asks my husband later. 'I wasn't really thinking of anything,' I replied, 'I just was.' I realised too how rare that is, just to be – utterly present to what is, and to ask for nothing more than that moment of mountain, bog, sky and lake and the sheer joy of being alive.

Seeing the dolphins

HAVING WATCHED AND WAITED MANY SUMMERS TO SEE dolphins in the bay near where we stayed, but with no success, I had finally learned to let go of the desire. My holiday was no longer punctuated by sighs of wishing for something other than what was given – for sun when it was stormy, for wild seas when it was calm, for dolphins when there were seals.

Then one morning in a different place I woke early and went to walk the beach, as usual, before breakfast. I had just started on my way back up when, for no reason that I could fathom, I turned round again for a last look, and they were there: six dolphins with that extraordinarily graceful movement turning in the waters. My heart leapt as I watched, and I was filled with delight. I also knew then that never again would I scan the waters wondering whether this shape or that might be a dolphin – they are so clearly themselves they cannot be mistaken for anything else. I also learned that you cannot command their appearance; dolphins, like grace, come unbidden and unexpected, and not because we want to see them.

Some months later we returned and one evening the sea was still as glass and silvered in the low sun. I was idly glancing out the window when those unmistakeable shapes cut through the water. I ran from the house to see them, three pairs curving up and under with that undulating movement as if they themselves were the missing waves on the ocean. As I watched the black shiny bodies against the bright water, suddenly they leapt right up out of the sea.

Since then in different cottages and at different times we have again seen the dolphins: dancing in the bay one New Year's Day, gliding through the waters on an April morning, seen through the mist on a June evening. Each time the response is similar; repetition does not dull it: it is a moment of awe at these embodiments of grace.

Listening for geese

I DON'T KNOW WHEN MY FASCINATION WITH BRENT GEESE began, but for the past number of years I've looked forward to their arrival in November and tried to visit their haunts regularly until their departure in March. I can't remember what struck me first. Was it seeing the large flock feeding, heads like question marks, poised on plump bodies? Was it when they flew overhead with their haunting cry? Was it the grace and shape of their flight in the sky? Was it the fact that they had travelled such a long way – from high-Arctic Canada – to get here?

Several years ago, feeling nervous about an impending teaching trip to Australia, I went to walk the beach in Wicklow and look for the geese. We'd gone the whole length of the shore but of the geese there was no sign. We were just turning back when I heard the familiar sound. I looked up and the sky was darkened with hundreds of beating wings flying just above our heads. The anxiety lifted and the fly-past of the geese felt like a blessing.

Six weeks later, when I returned home, one of the first places I visited was that same shore, and the geese were now getting ready for their own long-distance journey.

I watched again as they rose into the sky and it was now my turn to give the blessing.

Coming and going

THERE IS SOMETHING ABOUT BEING NEITHER HERE NOR there that is freeing. As one watches other travellers, one quickly becomes aware of those for whom the journey is a necessary means to an end: they watch the clock, impatient of any delay, irritated by the crying infant in the seat behind, oblivious to the anxiety of the old lady taking her first flight to visit her dying sister in a far-off country. There are others for whom the journey is part of the adventure. They come equipped with food and drink, and stories to hear and share. Their eyes are eager as they search out the new experiences, and across the aisle they proffer bread and grapes.

Some are anxious, all their belongings gathered in untidy heaps around them; children cling uncertainly to adults who are too preoccupied to notice them. Some are distressed. Some flee from places of war or famine. Others take flight to places of fantasy. Some, like Lot's wife, cannot journey at all – they can only look back in anger, nostalgia or in tears.

Then there are the stages in the journey, and that particular moment when one shifts from leaving to arriving, from going to coming, from ascending to descending, from taking off or setting out, to touching down, to coming in.

'Where have you come from? And where are you going?' the angel asked Hagar in the book of Genesis. The questions have haunted us ever since.

Arrivals

IN THOSE DAYS WHEN I USED TO COLLECT MY HUSBAND from the airport returning from regular trips to visit his mother in Cambridge, I tended to arrive early. He was puzzled. 'You don't want to hang about,' he insisted, 'Airports are dreadful places.' Well yes, if you are waiting for a flight and 'Delayed' flashes up on the screen, but I am fascinated by the arrivals.

I sit waiting and watching. There is the occasional French or Spanish exchange student looking sheepishly for a family holding a sign reading 'Colombe' or 'Pablo'. Awkward handshakes follow and slightly wary looks are exchanged as two young people size one another up. Small children are thrust forward to greet visiting grandparents; parents wait edgily wondering if they will recognise their own offspring. Summer visitors are welcomed with hugs and kisses and laughter. The regular business travellers walk brusquely past as if needing to disassociate themselves from this show of emotion.

Are these embraces because of long absences or simply the ordinary greeting of other family members returning from a holiday? The red legs and straw hats suggest a trip to somewhere exotic or at least sunny. For the travellers, the ritual of the greeting at the airport is vital. It confirms them in their sense that they have been on holiday and stepped out of the ordinary. They have the stripes to prove it.

On one occasion the waiting group was exceptionally large, carrying welcome signs, flowers and gifts. Then a cheer went up from the group and I saw a young couple coming through carrying a baby. Soon they were immersed in a sea of hugs and 'oohs' and 'ahs'. A woman turned to explain that her daughter was bringing home a baby she had adopted in China, and the whole family had come to welcome the new arrival. I found myself caught up in this surge of joy and was startled when a tap on my shoulder reminded me of my purpose. I turned to greet my husband, who was surprised when he received more than the perfunctory kiss.

Fear and flying

I DON'T LIKE FLYING. I HAVE TO PSYCHE MYSELF UP EACH time. The idea that this gigantic fuel-filled tin box can rise up in the sky and carry us across lands and oceans never ceases to amaze me.

Each time I fly I make an act of faith. Each time I arrive I breathe out my gratitude.

I have learned to imagine the currents of the air as if they were waves of the sea and I find myself quietly mouthing – 91:

> He shall cover you with his pinions,
> under his wings you will find refuge ...
> He will command his angels to guard you,
> on their hands they will bear you up.

But I begin to realise that this act of faith is simply an enlarged version of the trust that we need each day to live.

Fear paralyses. Fear holds me to the ground.

Faith lets me fly.

We visit friends in Gettysburg and discuss new presidents and new hopes.

'Look,' K. says, pointing to the sky, 'there are your geese.' I look up, as I often do at home, and marvel at the geese making their long journeys of migration, and recall the poet Moya Cannon as she reflects on our common needs 'to nest and to journey'.*

* From a poem entitled 'Migrations' in the collection, *Carrying the Songs* (Manchester: Carcanet Press, 2007), 111

Falling leaves

AUTUMN IS A STRANGE TIME: SO FULL OF BEAUTY WITH falling leaves and colours of reds and golds and oranges; of slanting light with the sun getting lower in the sky – and yet autumn is full of dying. We walk through woods or down streets when the wind catches those leaves and covers us in a rain-like shower. Children and foolish middle-aged women kick the leaves and dance. It is not until some weeks later when the trees are bare that we realise we were rejoicing in the dying. We pick up one of the fallen leaves and take it home, marvelling at the richness of its colour, but in a short few hours we will have discarded the dry shrivelled thing. We sweep it up along with the litter that has cluttered the path.

These are the paradoxes of our lives: the beauty and the dying, the beauty *of* the dying, the perfect and the imperfect together. After a summer of disturbance and disillusion when all that once seemed so glorious and full of promise has withered before our eyes, we might need to embrace autumn. In fact the American term might be even more appropriate – we need 'the fall'. Allowing ourselves to fall and to die may be, or rather is the only way towards new life, towards new hope, towards Resurrection.

Winter gardens

IT WAS EARLY JANUARY WHEN WE WALKED AROUND THE garden of a large estate. At first it seemed surprising that it would be open to the public at this time. But slowly we came to see a different beauty to summer lushness or autumn richness. As we walked among bare trees, we saw broad vistas made possible precisely because the skeleton black branches, which traced the grey-white sky, did not occlude the view.

There were brown and withered stalks in the herbaceous borders and seed heads, some as austere as contemporary sculptures. Yet in all of this there was a beauty, both in the apparent barrenness and in the promise: earth holding seeds and shoots waiting for the light of spring to re-create, to burst forth again.

Back in my own garden I thrill at the sight of the first snowdrop.

Planting bulbs seems such an act of trust in any case. It requires an effort to push each unpromising-looking brown and wrinkled bulb into the earth, and then patience to wait for months until first the green shoots and then the flowers appear. And being a rather haphazard gardener I can never quite remember where I planted the bulbs so am always surprised to see where they have come up and what has survived the nibbles of mice or the ravages of snails.

When we moved into our house, over twenty-five years ago, I planted crocuses with my young daughter around the base of an old apple tree. The tree is sadly gone, the child well grown, but each year the magic circle of crocuses appears and the flowers open to the sun for my daughter's February birthday.

Lent springing up

THE WORD LENT COMES FROM AN OLD ENGLISH WORD meaning spring. (This definition is still held in the common name for *Helleborus orientalis* as the Lenten rose, or the daffodil as the Lent lily.) My dictionary of Liturgy considers that this definition is now obsolete and has no relevance for the understanding of Lent as forty days of fasting in preparation for Easter, which takes its significance from the biblical forty days of Moses in the wilderness and Jesus in the desert.

Can both meanings not be held together to help heal that apparent rift between creation and redemption? In this hemisphere the cycle of ritual memory and of nature meet. As we enter the forty days of desert, nature is insisting vehemently on life's return. As we learn, through liturgical patterns, that unless a seed falls to the ground and dies it cannot live, nature illustrates the process.

Lenten days, spring days, are full of promise. The earth renews itself and the prayer of the psalmist is echoed:

> Create in me a clean heart O God,
> and put a new and right spirit within me.
> —Psalm 51:10

Picking damsons in September

The damsons are grey blue, with an almost velvet
   sheen,
in the early morning light.
They dot the trees of the orchard by the river
and mark the ground like bruises where they fall.
My shoes are wet through with the dew on the
   grass.
A crazy cat leaps into a tree, its weight sending
   down a branch within my reach.
I move from tree to tree and pick and fill my
   basket.
Later I carry the full basket carefully to the car.

Once home I sort and sift the hard, now darkened
    fruit.
I place the large pot on the stove.
Soon the whole house is filled with the autumn
    smell
of jam-making.
The damsons break down and soften, sending their
    stones to the surface,
to be taken out with a slotted spoon.
And my hands
are stained
purple.

Seeing the geese

IT WAS DECEMBER – ONE OF THOSE BRIGHT CRISP DAYS. WE
were doing that annual duty of Christmas shopping. I
remember that I had bags in both hands, because I wanted
to point to the sky and I had to put them down.

We were on our way home, exhausted, as you are when
you've made the twenty-sixth purchase of hat or gloves or
book or CD or tasteful bauble or bangle that you think your
third cousin twice removed would really like for Christmas.

We were heading for home.

None of this really matters because it was then I heard
them first. I looked up, and flying above the city streets

were hundreds of geese. They were probably on their way from one feeding ground to another – it was lunchtime after all. I called out in surprise and delight. We stood still almost in the middle of the road, oblivious now to everything but the geese brushing dark wings against the blue sky. We watched as flock after flock passed by in their distinctive V formation with that characteristic cry, which now we could make out clearly, even above the noise of the traffic. Like a street evangelist I wanted to tell everyone the good news of what I had seen, but all around me heads remained lowered and people rushed on, unaware of the wonder above them.

Exhaustion forgotten, we boarded the tram.

Now, one year later, I cannot remember one single thing we bought that day. But I remember the geese. I remember the joy, the utterly unexpected joy of seeing them there high above the streets, stringing out across the winter-pale sky.

PARABLES OF FAITH
AND FOLLY

There is perhaps always something foolish about faith, particularly in a secular time, but better to know one's own folly than to claim too much wisdom, better to be doubtful than righteous, better to practise than to preach, better to insert oneself into well-worn and well-trodden traditions than to invent one's own small gods.

Here and there in this collection I have woven in parables that find ways of retelling some familiar gospel stories, usually from the perspective of women whose voices are seldom heard or who are too often seen as marginal footnotes to the main text. These retellings give them a trace in the tradition.

I refer to them as parables rather than proofs because it seems to me that faith does not belong in the same realm as scientific proofs but rather in the place of the graced imagination where the heart is lifted and turned to the depths and mysteries of life.

All the pieces try to retain the idea of feet planted firmly on the ground while the eyes still search the skies for stars or plumb the depths for small wonders in unexpected places. Once again I juxtapose sacred and secular; for example one might expect to find 'grace' in a monastery but be surprised by it in a jazz club in New York city. The last piece, in tune with the tone and shape of the whole collection, returns our attention to the luminous in the ordinary as we once again find ourselves at the table for the breaking and blessing of bread.

God of the Gaps

PEOPLE USED TO TALK OF THE GOD OF THE GAPS – GOD AS the answer to our inability to explain the world. The concept is still alive in the idea that eventually scientists will 'know the mind of God'. This is an odd sort of God, God as filler, as construct of human inadequacy. It is reductionist and ultimately redundant. It's just one of the many gods I don't believe in.

American writer Annie Dillard has a very different perception of the God of the Gaps. She invites us to go into the gaps, those places of creeks and valleys where the winds pour down, where 'the icy fjords split the cliffs of mystery' and you cower to see 'the back parts of God'.* I love that phrase. I like its irreverence and the way it makes so ridiculous the whole notion of 'knowing the mind of God'. It refuses us the cosy comfort of a God caught in neat formulae of prayer or theology but offers instead a God to wrestle with, like Jacob with the angel, until at last, wounded, we just might receive a blessing.

The temptation is to resist that invitation and instead accept answers to questions we have not even begun to ask. Faith becomes a matter of assent rather than quest.

The gaps close over. The moment of possible transcendence vanishes and we settle for a god made in our own image, god writ small, god as the answer and not the question.

* Annie Dillard, *Pilgrim at Tinker Creek* (New York: Harper Perennial, 1974), 269

The visiting preacher

HE WAS YOUNG AND FRESH-FACED, FULL OF CONFIDENCE, our visiting preacher. His black robes hung in neat folds and his arms were enveloped in the voluminous sleeves. His sermon was perfectly constructed with appropriate rhetorical flourishes, his voice rose and fell as he emphasised certain points. His subject was redemption and the oxymoron of the *felix culpa*: where sin abounds there grace abounds more fully. He cited philosophers and theologians and impressed us with his learning and yet managed to contain his words precisely within the allotted ten minutes, for which the restless choirboys were deeply grateful.

And what was the verdict afterwards among the grey-haired elders of the congregation? A good sermon certainly, but let us hear him again when life's experiences have roughened those smooth edges. Call him back in ten or twenty years when he has experienced the grey desolation of God's absence. Then he can speak to us of faith. Call him back when he has suffered the wounds of rejection and failure. Then he can speak to us of loss and pain. Call him back when the polished words are dented by doubts. Then he can speak to us of hope and love.

The readers

IT WAS PALM SUNDAY AND A WOMAN STOOD UP TO NARRATE the Gospel. She had none of the 'elocution' vowels of someone trying too hard to impress. What was striking was that she read almost as if she was reading the newspaper. This sounds derogatory, but it is not meant to be. Mark writes with a kind of immediacy that suits that style. You expected her to stop at any moment and comment, 'Imagine that!' or 'The poor man – how could they treat him in that way?' As I stood in that church I closed my eyes and listened to an ancient story brought alive in the most unpretentious way. The reader never stumbled although she almost never paused – it was as if this was too interesting and she had to know what happened next, and yet it wasn't rushed. She was living this story and so were we.

The following Holy Thursday, in another church, a member of the congregation, who happens to be a poet, was one of the readers. I was struck by how this reader attended to the first reading from Exodus, also beautifully proclaimed, as if this would shape him for his own reading to follow. His head was bent forward and his ear inclined. He then stood and leaned into the microphone (the small voice) and spoke as intimately as if to one other. It was as if he had the most precious gift to impart, which of course he had: 'For this is what I received from the Lord, and in turn passed on to you ...'. The church was packed for the ceremony and yet there was total attention as we sat arrested by the voice of one bringing us words of life. I recalled hearing a friend of mine comment on a reading: 'It was wonderful to hear this read from the inside as it were.' In this case you felt that you were listening to someone who had meditated deeply before he opened his mouth. It was as if his own gifts with language had honed his attention to these words.

I realised after that week that I recalled almost nothing that had been said by any of the homilists but the readings remained in my inner ear for a long time. There are other times when the homily matters, but in that week the role of the celebrant is more akin to that of the leader of an orchestra. They have to allow these great liturgies to open our hearts and minds and this happens when profound attention is given both to reading and to ritual.

They are not to be explained but to be voiced.

Not telling but showing

SOME ART GALLERIES SEEM TO HAVE THE SAME POLICY AS fast food restaurants: get them in and out as quickly as possible. Make room for the next tour. Not so the small gallery in Siena next to the Duomo   here they provide chairs that you can pull up and stay and look, rather than pass through and tick off.

We have come to see Duccio's *Maesta* but in fact we spend most of the time looking at what would have been on the back of this large painting of the Virgin in majesty, originally an altarpiece. What interests us is the series of small pictures telling the story of the Passion.

We sit undisturbed for a long time, and looking at each scene in turn we tell the story again, the story so familiar and yet always other. We are particularly engaged by the dramatic showing of the denial of Peter. Duccio places this scene of Peter's denial, that he too was a follower of the Nazarene, directly beneath the courtroom scene, where Jesus faces his accusers. Downstairs the interlocutor is a maid; upstairs he is a high priest. Downstairs the maid points the finger at Peter. Upstairs the Christ figure stands before Annas. By the time of the third denial Peter is shown outside the very door where Christ is being beaten and the maid pierces him with her look. Above them is the crowing cock.

Just as we are about to leave a young Italian guide arrives with some visitors. With enthusiasm she begins to tell the story to her listeners. You would hardly need one word of Italian as her gesticulations and expressions demonstrate the betrayal of Judas, the denial of Peter. For a moment it is as if the unnamed maid of the painting has come to life, so immediate is this young woman's response to the unfolding drama.

We are transfixed and wish we could import her to some of our churches on Sundays, where those narratives have shrivelled up and dried out. That young girl could make an ancient painting, and an even older story, live again.

A new Pentecost

PARTHIANS, MEDES AND ELAMITES; PEOPLE FROM MESO-
potamia, Judea, Cappadocia, Pontus and Asia, Phrygia and
Pamphylia ... we hear them preaching in our own language
about the marvels of God (cf. Acts 2:10-11).

Amir, Abada, Abaya, Abayomi, Abdelwala, Abimbole,
and Abu now sit alongside the more familiar Abbot, Acton,
Adams.

Baader, Baalem, Babayev and Babel jostle with Bennett,
Burke and Byrne.

And before Zavislak, Zakas, Zhang and Zhon arrived,
did we even need to go as far as the letter Z?

I had picked up the telephone directory to check a
number and make a call and realised that it was as full of
potential narratives as any other bible. I ran my fingers
down the list of unfamiliar names and was brought back to
myself as a child struggling to read the lesson at Pentecost
and stumbling over the strange words.

And where have these people come from, I wondered?
What is their story?

I read their names and realised, perhaps more clearly than
ever before, that now their names are written in this book, they
are becoming part of the story of what this country is and will
be. I thought too of the alphabetical equality of the ordering
of the list of names, equality not often realised elsewhere.

The names in the book though signal at least a belonging,
a home here, an address, a place from which they go out

and come in, a place where who they are and where they have come from is recorded and may in time become a history of belonging.

Monastic life

IS THE CURRENT ATTRACTION TO THE MONASTIC LIFE AN indication of a desire to escape from the world or is it something else, possibly the desire to know the world more fully and engage with it at another level? There is a marked increase in the numbers joining such communities, as well as in the numbers of visitors coming to make retreats, 'to taste and see'.

This has been my first visit of this nature and I have fallen for all the clichés to describe the experience: silence, solitude, peace, simplicity and so on – and this despite the fact that I was rudely awoken on my first morning by the most raucous noise of the rooks. There seem to be so many more hours in the day with the benefit of the early rise for matins. 'Everything is relative,' commented the abbot, 'I had the same feeling when I was visiting a sister monastery where they rose at 3.30 a.m.'

The day is punctuated by prayers and meals and there is, paradoxically, a sense of freedom in the set routine. You eat what is set before you, you pray when summoned by the bells, all very soothing. For now it has a liberating effect, freeing one from the tyranny of choice. And perhaps in time, having somehow transcended the monotony of the routine, it could also become a rhythm as natural as breathing, a habit, not of serge, but of the heart. I wonder whether there is even a tiny vestige of this that I could retain.

Perhaps I could learn to greet the morning with 'O Lord, open thou my lips and my mouth will speak forth your praise' rather than, 'O God, it's not that time again!'

The sounds of silence

EVERYONE WHO COMES TO THE MONASTERY COMMENTS ON the silence. But is it silence, I wonder, or is it in fact the ability to listen? We hear again because our ears are no longer assaulted from all sides with an almost constant cacophony of sounds. Here the sounds separate themselves and can be distinguished.

You hear the toll of the bell calling the monks to prayer, swiftly followed by the sound of feet moving along the passageway to the church. You listen to the short readings or the rhythmic chanting of the psalms in a liturgy where there is no silence until after the last blessing. Then there is the sound of meals eaten in silence. You listen to the instructions: 'Supper is eaten in the refectory with the monks.' 'We will process in together; then there is the grace; when everyone is seated food is served.' 'There will be a reading.' It is surprisingly easy not to have to engage in conversation at the table; yet another source of stress is lifted. There is no 'proving oneself' here, no explanations;

one is simply present, that is enough. But not speaking does not mean total silence. It means different noises. Perhaps as a novice to the experience, if not the way of life, I am aware of knives and forks on plates, robes swishing as the serving monks move up and down the room, dishes being swiftly cleared away, the odd cough, chairs pulled back as the thanksgiving grace is said.

When I come down to breakfast one morning I find myself alone, and then I am struck by the absence of the usual noises: no traffic outside, no radio screaming its commercials at me, no television in the corner. But there are other sounds: the raucous rooks that had woken me earlier have quietened and now I hear the robin and the thrush. When I walk down the avenue there is a honking sound and I look up to see that the swans have lifted into the air. A car racing past rudely disturbs the peace. Later on my return I find a dead thrush, as yet untouched, probably having been stunned by the car, a reminder, if I needed one, that this is not paradise – it is another way of living in the same flawed world.

Sketches of grace in the city

WE PAID A VISIT TO NEW YORK ONE AUTUMN, AND ON THIS, our second visit, I found myself less overawed and more attuned to the small forms of life among those skyscrapers.

Central Park was turning to its winter colours in majestic manner but this time we found a 'secret garden', a small oasis, with a notebook in a glass case where you could pencil in any sightings of birds or butterflies.

This time it was less about the exotic places to eat, but more about the small cafés where women brought laptops and revised their novels or wrote their journals, or where the waitress from Slovakia brought an extra portion because my husband reminded her of her father.

Last time it was fun to ride in yellow cabs. This time it was good to travel on the subway. A homeless man slept, his head resting on the shoulder of a reading girl. She didn't move until it was her stop, whereupon she gently extricated herself.

At an exhibition of Van Gogh's night paintings a small child counted the stars for his grandmother. At a play on Broadway a daughter rushed out at the interval to buy a pashmina shawl for five dollars from a stall for her mother. Thus fortified against the cool of the air conditioning the pair enjoyed the heat of the dialogue.

I still don't know where Macy's is but I do know where you can buy the best rye bread I have ever tasted.

We don't visit Wall Street where stockbrokers are gnashing their teeth, but in a small club a jazz musician, who had been gravely ill and can barely speak, plays the piano for his friends, and men weep and take his face in their hands and tenderly embrace him and thank him for the gift of his music.

Candidates for compassion

THE BURDEN OF CARING FOR HIS ELDERLY AND ILL FATHER-in-law in a cramped Bombay flat is too much for Yezad, a character in the novel by Indian writer Rohinton Mistry, with the gently punned title, *Family Matters*. Yezad distances himself and refuses to participate in the routine of feeding, changing and cleaning the old man, all of which is leaving his wife exhausted.

Then one day he finds himself bringing over the feeding cup with tea to 'the chief', as he calls him. He is taken aback at how long it takes to give him the drink, but when he is finished his father-in-law lays his shaking hand over that of his son-in-law and their two hands tremble as they hold the cup together. Yezad then proceeds to cut his father-in-law's toenails and to shave him.

How can his wife do this all the time? he wonders. It isn't that she's used to it, he is sure of that; it must be love. The final breakthrough comes when Yezad, with the help of his two young sons, brings the bedpan and, overcoming his nausea, cleans up the chief.

He has finally come to understand his own observation of some weeks before when, watching his father-in-law, he noted: 'Curious ... how if you know a person long enough he would elicit every kind of emotion from you, every possible reaction, envy, admiration, pity, irritation, fury, fondness, jealousy, love, disgust. But in the end all human beings become candidates for compassion, all of us without exception ... and if we could recognise this from the beginning what a saving in grief and misery.'*

* London: Faber, 2002, 348

Feeling sorry ...

IN LUKE'S GOSPEL WE FIND A STORY OF JESUS RAISING THE son of the widow of Nain (7:11-17). Like all good stories it is told with disarming simplicity: 'Jesus went to a town called Nain accompanied by his disciples and a great number of people ... It happened that a dead man was being carried out for burial, the only son of his mother and she was a widow ... When the Lord saw her he felt sorry for her ... "Do not cry," he said, and he went and put his hand on the bier and the bearers stood still. "Young man I tell you to get up."'

I am puzzled by the phrase, 'He felt sorry for her'.

You feel sorry for someone if they miss the bus, if they have a cold, if it rains on their washing, or their wedding ... but this is a matter of life and death.

Some translations use the word 'compassion'. This is closer to the original. Compassion means to 'suffer with'. It is an act of graced imagination. It draws one out of the stupor of self-centredness into a revelatory moment of being with another. Compassion breaks through the strictures of law and righteousness, of codes of ethics or rituals of purity.

If Jesus had merely felt sorry for the widow, as we feel sorry for women and men who daily lose their sons and daughters in war or famine, then Jesus, like us, would have uttered some pious prayers and passed on. He didn't feel sorry – he had *compassion* for the widow and so her life was transformed, her son's life was restored.

The prodigal son

YOU KNOW THAT STORY IN THE GOSPEL OF LUKE WHERE the youngest son asks for his share of the inheritance and takes off to experience the world outside his small village ...

We never hear about the mother – she doesn't get a mention. Well, I know how she feels. She worries about her son. She wakes in the night and thinks about him. She can't even hope for an email or a text. She knows they had to let him go because from the moment he was born she realised that the whole business of love was about letting go. She knows in her heart that he's a good lad; he'll do foolish things of course, get into all sorts of trouble, but he'll learn and grow. He was always curious about the world, her youngest – always interested in difference, in the variety and spices of life. (He may bring back some of those too.) He'll have spent more than his allowance, she's sure of that. He'll come back with nothing but the clothes he's standing in, but she won't care; she'll just want him back – and safely.

She feels sure that one day he will return, and that when he does his father won't be able to hold back his joy. He'll run towards him when he sees his son coming and he'll embrace him and throw his arms around him and throw a party for him. Funny, she thinks, how people go on about the wasteful 'sinful' life of the boy in that parable; she doesn't think that's the point at all: it's really about the extravagant prodigal love that abounds and abides, always ready to forgive and embrace. She knows that. He is the child of her womb.

She realises that he will have changed, that boy, that he will now be a man who has known pain and joy, great loneliness and wonderful companionship. She knows too that the relationships in the household will shift to accommodate the returned traveller, no longer a child dependent on them, but one who will bring his wisdom and experience into the exchange of love.

The lamb will be roasted; his father will see to that. She will make a loaf of brown bread.

Shades of grey

'WHO ARE THE BADDIES?' ASKED THE SMALL CHILD watching cartoons.

Once reassured as to who the bad guys were he could relax and enjoy the tension of the story. For the child the world is safer when divided into black and white, good and bad. As he grows he may, with any luck but more likely through painful experience, discover that living is less simple: that things, far from being 'black and white', come in many shades of grey. He will learn that morality is a maze and you have to discern the good by carefully, carefully sifting.

Thus the child may become a thinking adult.

This will be helped by reading novels, by going to the cinema and the theatre, by looking at art, as much or more than reading tomes on ethics or law, or learning the ten or one-hundred-and-ten commandments. However, the child who has never been exposed to things that stretch her imagination and open her eyes of understanding may become one who is quick to judge, who condemns easily, who refuses compassion.

That child may become a man who cannot face his own imperfections, who perhaps was never allowed to fail, who cannot bear to see the weakness of others. For their weakness is a mirror in which he cannot afford to look, lest it looks back at him, and he sees his less than perfect self.

Such a child becomes an adult, ill-equipped to deal with the world – the messy, muddled, often brutal, but sometimes graced, world in which they, in which we, need to live.

Always someone to blame

SIN HAS BEEN BLOTTED OUT.

And I'm not talking about redemption, or even confession and forgiveness of sin. Now there is no sin to forgive: no personal weakness, no failing, no falling short.

There are mistakes of course. Things go wrong.

People and computers crash. But usually someone else is to blame.

Start with our parents: they gave too much or too little love.

But one way or another they messed us up (Philip Larkin put it more graphically). Then our teachers: if we are over fifty they were too strict, beat some of us, scarred all of us, rendered us less perfect than we might have been. If we are under forty they were too lenient, they gave us no guidelines, no maps for living.

Then of course there's always the Church, with a capital C, to blame for most things, telling us what to do, making a right mess of it themselves.

And now the media – the new high priests. They too carry much responsibility: the hard-line righteousness coming from the expected 'fuming fundamentalists' and more surprisingly the apparently 'liberal' left. They are good at judging and shaming, passing sentence without mercy.

Yes, there's always someone to blame for the cracks on the pavement, for the cracks we slip through.

Original sin

I'VE DISCOVERED A SURE WAY OF STOPPING CONVERSATION at a dinner party: introduce the topic of original sin. I know; I tried it. Until that moment conversation had flowed, and we were now discussing recent events in the media – inevitably involving the fall from grace, or position, of some politician or personality. We talked about society's need to judge, condemn, humiliate – particularly those whom it had recently praised and raised. The drive for perfection, upon which we insist, demands its counterpart – the darkness that exists outside of us, somewhere else, someone else, to be condemned.

I was trying to say something about the need to accept that we are all flawed, born into a broken, fragile world and that this awareness of the fault lines is the meaning of 'original sin'.

They weren't having any of it. To them it evoked all the unpleasantness of an authoritarian Church imposing this concept on us.

No, I tried to say, it didn't impose this. It named what was there: our tendency to false illusion, to false promise, to hurt and be hurt, to wound and be wounded, to fail and be failed.

But I failed too … and someone poured more wine, and then it began to snow, and someone else said we should read James Joyce's *The Dead*.

And as the guests left the snow was drifting down … falling softly; they disappeared into its stillness and its whiteness …

The scapegoat

THEY SAY THAT JUDAS IS UP FOR REHABILITATION. POOR
old Judas – he has had rather a bad press.

Why, I wonder, has no one pitied him?

Why did the lines 'and he went and hanged himself',
cause only further condemnation and no compassion?

Did Peter too not betray Jesus?

Did Judas not repent?

Was he not overcome by utter despair?

Is there no forgiveness for that?

Does the mercy of God not stretch beyond the limits of
death, beyond the limits of our imaginations?

Is there not a moment of poignancy in the narrative,
when Judas tries to return the tainted money, and they will
not take it back?

'What is that to us?' they say.

He has served his purpose, is of no further use to them.

Do we not recognise any of our frailties here?

Instead we take our anger, our failings and our betrayals
of one another and place them onto the back of Judas.

Let him carry them.

Let him be our scapegoat.

We're good at that kind of thing, one of the things we
do best in fact – demonising the other.

They stand in the shadow that we might stay in the
light.

Folly: Summer 2006[*]

Hot, dry July.
The silly season of hats and horses.

Bombs dropping on Lebanon,
over one thousand dead.

Long delays at airports,
no hand cream allowed on board.
Someone is mocking this madness.

No ceasefire called.

'War against terror.'
'Axis of evil.'
Women and children
run screaming from their homes.
Did no one explain the fine distinctions to them?

Precision bombs drop randomly,
killing messengers on bikes,
and men delivering bread.

War against terror.
Terrifying, terrorising war.
Tell me, is there any other kind?

Women are weeping in Israel,
burying dead soldiers, their sons.
Men are burying women and children in Lebanon.

Why does everything in us
not protest this barbarism?
Why is such expertise put at the service of such
    destruction?
Who decides when enough have died,
when enough is destroyed,
when enough are displaced?

Why are we silent? Why are we ...?
Why are ...?
Why ...?

* This was composed in 2006 but remains sadly relevant in 2014

Prayers of the faithless

From prayers which cover all eventualities, O God,
    preserve us.
For all who are sick, all who are poor, all out of work, all
refugees, all victims of war or famine, all the dying, all
the living.

From the long lists of the long dead, save us we pray.

From prayers which give too much information, O God,
    preserve us.
From knowing the name of the child who died when a
    bomb hit her village, O God, preserve us.
From knowing the names of the forty-nine others who
    died when a bomb hit their village, O Lord, save us,
    we pray.

From knowing the names of the children who perished
    from famine, save us, we pray.
From knowing the names of the mothers and fathers
    who could not feed them, prevent us.
From too much unbearable reality, O Lord, come to our
    aid.

God of the faithless, hear us we pray.

Too much God

IF I STAYED TOO LONG IN SMALL-TOWN AMERICA, I THINK
I would quickly join the ranks of the non-religious. I would
wish that American presidents would invoke the name of
God less often. Many things have been done in 'God's
name', and some degree of reticence about using God-talk
would be salutary.

I attended one church where the celebrant was female
but God was definitely male, for when she called on him,

'HE' replied with a booming deep voice through the loudspeakers to encourage the congregations to give more money while assuring the pastor that 'she was doing a good job'. Everything belonged to God, we were told, and had to be given back, although it looked as if the pastor got to decide what to do with God's money.

It struck me that certain words like 'God' and 'morality' have become totem-like. They are spat out and require no elucidation. They have actually ceased to operate as means of communication and instead have become full stops to conversation. 'God' used in that way is a dead letter, not a living word.

I'm going to hazard a guess that most truly religious people concern themselves very little with God writ large. It is not belief in this apparently immovable object that concerns them, but rather the way the word becomes vulnerable flesh in the world.

There was once a woman …

IN THESE DAYS WHEN LITERALISTS SEEK TO PIN DOWN texts, and holy, holy scriptures from all sides are used as weapons of destruction, it is a relief to turn to parables. Parables are those tales told in the gospels, usually by Jesus, when someone is trying to trap him. We live in a litigious society. He did too. Words were dangerous then. They are now. Words can be taken out of context and your olive branch becomes a stick to beat you with.

Parable, from the Greek, suggests throwing one thing alongside another, so that the mind is teased to explore possible meanings. Parable is more play than preaching, more poetry than prose.

Luke tells a tale about a woman who has ten coins and loses one and spends all day searching for it. When she finds it she invites the friends and neighbours in. The woman is the first surprise. It is her house. She is the subject of the story, and not as so often the object.

The second surprise is the money business. You might expect that spiritual teaching would be about spiritual things. Should there be such a fuss about money? Well, she needs to live: one tenth of her probably meagre savings has been lost.

The third surprise is her way of praying. She doesn't fall to her knees and implore St Anthony, or whoever looked after lost property in those days, to come to her aid. No, she lights a lamp, sweeps carefully, searches thoroughly.

There is one last surprise: having found the money, she blows it on a party for her friends and neighbours. And there was much rejoicing in heaven.

And you ask what God is like? Well, there was once a woman ...

Interrupting women

'WHERE DID I COME FROM?' IS ONE OF THE FIRST QUESTIONS of a small child. Depending on mood or circumstance the child will be told: you come from Mullingar, or Leitrim ... from Beijing or Lagos ... from under the gooseberry bush ... from the womb of your mother ... from good stock.

Matthew at the beginning of his gospel wants to root Jesus in the history of God's people so he gives a long genealogy of Jesus as son of David. Abraham was the father of Isaac ... Isaac the father of Jacob ... Jacob the father of Judah ... Judah the father of Perez ... and so on ... we are almost numbed by the long list of forefathers.

Yet into this list slip four women, Tamar, Rahab, Bathsheba and Ruth. According to commentators, these women are either of questionable morality, or outsiders. Is it not odd then to include them in this list written to establish the good stock of Jesus?

I am reminded of those who do research into their family origins and find both slaves and slave-owners, or convicts and prison-camp guards, betrayers and betrayed, abusers and abused, and have to come to terms with the ambivalence of their history.

Perhaps these women are included precisely because they interrupt the flow, because they defy the conventions of their society and yet God's plan flows through them.

Perhaps the pattern is broken because it is only through the brokenness of ordinary lives that grace is revealed, and in and through muddied, muddled human lives that God is made manifest.

Lost for words

'JUST TO SAY I'M BACK SAFELY FROM THE TREK. IT WAS awesome. Talk later.'

Thus went the text from our son letting us know that he was back in Darjeeling after a six-day trek in the Himalayan mountains.

Later that day I am working with a group discussing the role of women in the Gospel of Mark. We are debating the meaning of the abrupt ending: 'They said nothing to anyone for they were afraid.'

For a long time this has puzzled scribes and commentators. In fact, extra endings were tacked on as this one was considered so unsatisfactory.

Some say it proves that the women disciples are as flawed and faithless as the male disciples in that gospel, who desert and flee at the time of the Passion. Others say it demonstrates the unreliability of women witnesses. Some few acknowledge that 'fear' might be an appropriate response to the cataclysmic event that was resurrection.

I offer my son's text as an explanation: 'It was awesome. They couldn't speak.'

They would tell the story later – and they did – as the 'gossips' in the villages became the storytellers of the 'good news'.

Ordinary resurrection

ENOUGH OF EMPTY TOMBS AND DAZZLING ANGELS,
   enough of rending veils and hearts,
   enough of dumbstruck guards and stones rolled back,
   enough of incredulous men, and witnessing women,
   enough of quaking earth and dancing sun.

Some of us cannot take 'the overwhelming' of resurrection glory, our feet are clay-clogged, mud-stuck – this is all too much for us, we are looking for an ordinary miracle.

We know the pain of hopes dashed, expectations disappointed – with this we can identify. We too, like the downcast disciples on the road to Emmaus, would be glad of a stranger to walk with us in times of sorrow and talk with us until we began to see things differently.

We know what it feels like to be blinded by a sense of failure – to be locked in or locked out by the stone walls we ourselves have carefully made. The light that comes into that darkness, which is not death but is its kin, is the resurrection that we seek. We hope for the kind of angel who touched Elijah in his misery and insisted that he 'get up and eat'. This kind of angel is usually well disguised, the wings tucked in.

But if, and when, the scales fall from our eyes, it is not angels we will think of but that smile, that touch which restores life to the deadened, and yes, the smell and taste of her bread broken, blessed and shared.

POSTSCRIPT

A small wonder

You arrived in mid-summer – our first grandson.
Your mother (who had become a mother upon
    your arrival) held you out:
'Isn't he a perfect little creature?' she asked,
but the question was rhetorical,
and needed simply our assent.
'And look at his big hands.'
'Ah,' said his grandfather (on the musical side of
    the family)
'he'll play the harpsichord.'
'I knew you'd say that!' replied our daughter.
His other grandmother (on the medical side) will say:
'With those hands he'll be a surgeon.' And she did.
Your father (who had become a father upon your
    arrival) said,
'He can be both.'

Watching and listening to these exchanges this
    grandmother wondered what wish
or blessing to impart to you, and whether anything
    further was needed for one
born on the feast of St Bonaventure – the name
    already bringing 'good fortune'.
She thought of how every birth, every new life
    causes a surge of gratitude and joy to rise up in
    us.
'It's the endorphins released during birth,' says the
    scientist cousin, 'We all pick them up.'
Being more inclined to poetry (or prayer) she
    wants to say more than that.
She wants to sing out, or at least write down, how
    this 'perfect little creature', as your parents
    describe you, opens us again to 'wonder'. As
    she does, she begins to see that this is also what
    she wishes for you: that delight, curiosity and
    wonder about this world may stay with you: past
    the innocence of your childhood, into the tested
    experience of your growing up, and finally into
    the wisdom of your old age.

15 July 2014